DOGGY  PROBLEMS SOLVED

AMANDA O'NEILL

DOGGY  PROBLEMS SOLVED

How to stop your dog's embarrassing behaviour

INTERPET PUBLISHING

Published by
Interpet Publishing,
Vincent Lane,
Dorking,
Surrey RH4 3YX,
England

ISBN 978-1-84286-217-9

The recommendations
in this book are given
without any guarantees
on the part of the
author and publisher.
If in doubt, seek the
advice of a vet or pet-
care specialist.

The Author

Amanda O'Neill was born in Sussex in 1951 and educated at the University of Exeter, where she studied medieval literature. She has written more than 20 books, including *The Best-Ever Book of Dogs*, *What Dog?* and *DogBiz*, and she was the editor of *The Complete Book of the Dog*. She is also a regular contributor to a number of national dog magazines in the United Kingdom. She lives in the Midlands with her son and a pack of small dogs, mostly rescues.

Credits
Editor:
Philip de Ste. Croix
Designer:
Philip Clucas MSIAD
Cartoons:
Russell Jones
Index:
Richard O'Neill
**Production
management:**
Consortium, Suffolk
Print production:
1010 Printing
International Ltd,
China
Printed and bound
in China

INTRODUCTION

In the 21st century, dog ownership leads to more problems than ever before. Human lifestyles are more urban, more work-oriented and less dog-friendly. We expect dogs to fit into those lifestyles even if we are out at work all day and our leisure time is already taken up with childcare, cooking, socialising, etc. Anti-dog regulations increasingly limit where we can take our dogs and what we can do with them.

◀ *Big energetic working dogs may not be the best choice for urban life.*

In the age of the car, we walk far less in our daily lives than people used to and therefore have to set aside specific time for dog-walking — often underestimating our pets' exercise needs.

Often we choose the least suitable type of dog in the first place: we buy high-maintenance, working breeds as pets without taking their work instincts and energy into account, we misguidedly buy sickly, unsocialised puppies from puppy farms which may never overcome their developmental difficulties, we buy 'designer puppies' as fashion accessories *(right)* and then discover that dogs are higher-maintenance than handbags, or we adopt rescue dogs with tragic histories and expect to be able to repair their emotional damage in just a few months.

CONFUSING ADVICE

To add to the confusion, we are faced with a proliferation of experts and theories of dog behaviour, each of which is claimed to be the answer to all our doggy problems and yet which

▲ *Even a walk in the park often involves a drive in the car, so dogs need to learn good car manners.*

are often contradictory. We pick up helpful tips from assorted behaviour theories, only to find that these tips don't work as we expected — and some of them are downright dangerous. There was the fashion for choke chains, acceptable (though not ideal) training aids in the hands of an expert, but instruments of torture when incorrectly applied.

More recently we have had the hierarchical approach, holding that the dog owner has to be 'alpha dog' in the household, which led to all sorts of perfectly nice and undominant dogs being driven to bite as their owners insisted on 'asserting dominance' (otherwise known as bullying) by pinning them on their backs for no apparent reason (the 'alpha roll') and repeatedly taking their dinners away from them. Another 'helpful tip' that is often misused and abused is crate-training, intended to provide the dog with a safe and private shelter of his own, and all too often ending up as a prison cell where the poor dog spends hours in solitary confinement.

FIND A GOOD TRAINER

Do be aware that there is no one quick fix for behaviour problems. A method that works for one trainer may not work for another, because trainers, and dogs, are individuals. Some people are naturally talented dog trainers; most of us aren't, and have to learn from experience. A good local training class can be a real help, because it gives you (and your dog) the opportunity to learn from other people's experience too. However, it is vital to check out any training class before enrolling – ask if you can sit in on a session without your dog and observe before you commit yourself. Look for a class where the trainer obviously likes dogs, and where both owners and dogs are clearly enjoying the session. If the class employs choke chains, dominating methods or physical punishment, if the trainer doesn't engage with dogs or their owners, or if the dogs in the class seem tense and worried – run a mile. This sort of class isn't just unpleasant for all concerned, but is likely to make your dog's behaviour (and your own anxiety about it) worse.

You should also check out the aims of the class. Some are geared to competition-style obedience, which is not necessarily the same thing as the basic obedience desired by most pet-owners. (For example, most of us want a dog who comes when he is called; not many of us regard it as equally important that he should sit in exactly the right position when he arrives.) You should also be looking for a trainer who regards dogs, and their owners, as individuals, and aims to bring out the best in each rather than force them all to work in an over-standardised way.

◀ A crate can be a great training aid and a comfy refuge for your dog, but if not correctly introduced, it becomes a jail.
▶ Your dog will learn much more at his training class if he finds it a happy experience.

INTRODUCTION

If you don't live near a helpful training class or individual trainer, don't despair. Most behavioural problems can be improved by

1 Spending more time on training.
2 Providing your dog with more physical exercise.
3 Trying to 'think dog'.
4 Remembering that rewards work better than punishment.

Use the 'Off' command when appropriate.

▲ *Dogs learn as they follow you around the house. Make sure that what they learn is positive by incorporating lessons into your routine.*

TRAINING TIME

Allocating more time to training not only increases your dog's chances of learning but also helps to keep his mind occupied, reducing boredom, and encourages him to focus on you rather than on making his own entertainment. Little and often is a good general rule: ten minutes several times a day is likely to be more productive than an hour at the weekend. You can fit in all sorts of lessons around your daily routine. If you want to watch television in peace, that's the perfect time to practise a quiet 'Down stay'. If you're doing housework and the dog is following you around, there's your opportunity to fit in 'In' and 'Out' through various doors, 'Leave it' as he investigates various objects, 'Off' as he

hops on to chairs, and so on. If he brings you a toy, you can encourage him to 'Give', or work on his retrieves. The more time you spend on training, the better results you will obtain.

PHYSICAL EXERCISE

Most pet dogs are massively under-exercised. A working sheepdog may cover 100km (60 miles) a day – many pet collies have to be content with half an hour in the park. Insufficient exercise means surplus energy to be worked off, often in pursuit of mischief or challenging behaviour. Obviously not many pet-owners are in a position to walk marathons every day, but if you simply double your dog's daily exercise, he is more likely to be content to rest quietly at home instead of charging around wrecking the place.

Puppies are a special case. They have bursts of abundant energy (and mischief), which can't be worked off with long walks until they are old enough for their bodies to handle the exercise.

▲ *Schedule free-running periods, playing in the park or chasing a ball to use up energy.*

LEARN TO 'THINK DOG'	
How we may interpret a dog's behaviour	**What his behaviour actually means**
My dog follows me all round the house because he loves me so much.	He is over-dependent and insecure.
My dog snarls and lunges at passers-by because he wants to protect me.	He is scared of other people/strange situations.
My dog sits so close that he almost pushes me out of my chair because he is devoted to me.	He thinks he's boss and that you are subservient to him.
My dog doesn't do what I tell him because he thinks he is dominant over me.	He doesn't understand what you mean (communication failure on your part).

▶ *You need to understand how your dog's mind works if he is to understand you.*

Over-walking a young pup is likely to cause bone or tissue damage, so take care. A short walk or 15 minutes of robust play at a time is enough for baby puppies; build up exercise gradually until your pup is mature (remembering that larger breeds mature more slowly than small ones).

'THINKING DOG'

It's important to remember that dogs don't speak English and don't think the same way we do. Try and put yourself in his place to avoid mutual misunderstandings. It's all too easy to give your dog the wrong message. If your puppy picks up a sock and you chase after him to rescue it, he thinks you are joining in his game, not trying to stop it – better to ignore him and find a distraction, even if it means sacrificing one sock.

If he jumps on you with muddy paws and you shout at him, he thinks you are rejecting him rather than his dirty pawprints and may become reluctant to come to you again – better to ignore him and start teaching him to greet you with all four feet on the ground.

REWARDS NOT PUNISHMENT

Reward-based training is not only more pleasurable for both dog and owner, but also more productive. Punishment makes your dog slower to learn, reduces his trust in you and does nothing for his enthusiasm for learning. Your goal should be to have a dog who looks forward to training sessions and is keen to show you how clever he is, not one who hides behind a chair when the training lead appears.

Owning a dog should be a pleasure rather than a burden. Make it fun for your dog, and you will both reap the rewards.

◀ *Rewards aren't bribes, but a way of making it clear to your dog that he has done the right thing and that you are happy with him.*

FOOD FOUL-UPS

Food plays an important part in dogs' lives – sometimes too much so for owners' comfort. What our dogs eat and how they eat it are important to us, too. Common problems include dogs who make a nuisance of themselves over food, faddy feeders, and those who eat neither wisely nor too well.

MY DOG WON'T STOP EATING

Causes: Medical conditions such as diabetes; lack of other interests (boredom); learned behaviour arising from past under-feeding or over-feeding (e.g. excessive feeding of titbits); and of course some dogs are just plain greedy!

Breed notes: Some breeds are natural gluttons – most famously Labradors.

Action: See your vet to check out possible medical problems. If your dog is healthy, encourage him to take up other interests. Keeping him busy with play-time, walks and training will reduce the time he has for obsessing about food. At home, minimise his opportunities to scavenge food by dog-proofing waste bins, etc. (see below,

▼ Accessible waste bins are an open invitation to a dog – move them out of temptation's way.

Most dogs love junk food.

My Dog Steals Food). On walks, if necessary, control scavenging with an extending lead or a basket-type muzzle, and try to focus your dog's attention on play or training. Changing to a higher-fibre diet may help, as this will make your dog feel fuller after eating.

Prevention: Establish regular times for feeding (twice a day, in the early morning and early evening, will suit most dogs) and stick to them. Don't hand out treats at random, and if you use food rewards for training, be conscious of the total amount given. Try to avoid situations where food scavenging is a temptation, and make sure your dog has enough mental and physical stimulation to avoid 'boredom snacking'.

MY DOG STEALS FOOD

Dogs who raid garbage bins, jump up on the kitchen counter and learn to open food cupboards for self-service snacks can drive an owner mad – and put their own health at risk.

Causes: Medical conditions; boredom; opportunity; greed.

Action: Exclude any hunger-inducing medical cause before tackling the problem. Booby-trapping food (leaving out food on a pile of precariously balanced cans which will fall with a clatter when the dog tries to steal it) may discourage some individuals. However, tough-minded dogs will ignore the noise and sound-sensitive dogs can be distressed to the point of becoming food-phobic. More effective is the two-pronged approach: remove the opportunity for stealing, and introduce an acceptable replacement behaviour. **First**, make all food inaccessible. Fit cupboards with child-proof locks, move waste bins out of reach, never leave food on kitchen counters, and never leave the table unattended with food on it – if you have to get up from the table, take your plate with you. You can also block access to the kitchen with a nursery gate. While re-educating your dog, clean up all spills scrupulously so that he cannot help himself to so much as a crumb. It often helps to bribe children to clean up after themselves!

Secondly, introduce your dog to an alternative rewarding behaviour. Teach him to lie down, on a mat or in a particular corner, while you are preparing or eating meals, and reward him for doing so with a titbit. Initially, reward short periods of staying put, building up to the point where he understands what is required and will wait until you have finished.

Prevention: With a new puppy, follow the two-point programme from the start so that your dog never acquires bad habits.

▶ *Like children, dogs need to learn good table manners.*

MY DOG PESTERS US AT MEALTIMES

Cause: Your dog has learned that this technique works.

Action: Don't give in! Very often one member of the family lets the side down by feeding the dog at table, and half the battle lies in re-educating the human culprit. Teach your dog to go to his bed, or other approved site, while you are eating, taking him a small food reward for staying put when you have finished. At first you will have to get up from the table repeatedly to take him back to his station, until he has learned that food is only forthcoming when he lets you eat in peace. Be persistent and consistent to win the day.

Prevention: Stick to the above regime from the first day, even if your dog is sitting quietly by the table looking irresistible.

FOOD FOUL-UPS

MY DOG EATS ANIMAL DROPPINGS

To a dog, waste products are just part of life's rich menu. Droppings contain undigested food traces, which dogs are often happy to recycle. However, most owners are less happy with this habit, and it carries health risks, such as parasitic infestation.

Causes: Opportunity/learned behaviour; dietary deficiency; greed; attention-seeking.

Action: As a short-term measure, control your dog's access to smelly snacks by walking him on an extending lead and, if necessary, using a muzzle. At the same time, work on training. At home and on walks, practise recall and 'Leave it' commands, using rewards, until your dog is quite clear that abandoning his find pays off. If he does snatch up a mouthful of droppings, never chase him (which rewards his action with an enjoyable game) – try attracting his attention by running away instead. A high-fibre diet may help to reduce his appetite. You can also

try deterrent training: use an extending leash and, as soon as your dog approaches his goal, use training discs or a rattle can to put him off. Above all, the most useful tactic is to focus your dog's attention on you while on walks, using the time for positive interaction via games, training practice and rewards. You need to become more interesting than a pile of rabbit droppings!

Prevention: Don't make the surprisingly common mistake of ignoring your dog while on walks. Interacting with him is not only more fun, but enables you to nip bad habits like this in the bud. Working on the 'Leave it' command will also be beneficial.

MY DOG EATS HIS OWN FAECES

Causes: Opportunity/learned behaviour (prolonged kennelling or living as a stray can lead to this habit); stress/anxiety; boredom; dietary deficiency (due to poor diet or a medical condition preventing absorption of food); greed; attention-seeking.

Action: First of all, restrict access! Supervise toileting sessions, and be meticulous about picking up poop. Faeces should never be left lying around to attract your dog's attention. However, racing your dog to reach the mess first is likely to make him competitive and even keener, so instead call him away from temptation with a titbit as soon as he has squatted. Short-term use of a muzzle may be advisable with dogs who are obsessive about faeces-eating. Second, consider changing your dog's diet to make his faeces less palatable to him. Try switching from 'wet foods' to a good quality

▲ A muzzle will stop your dog snatching smelly snacks, but needs to be introduced gradually.

dry food, bulk out meals with bran or cooked greens, or simply add a few pineapple chunks to your dog's dinner.

Prevention: Always clear up your dog's messes before he has a chance to get interested. If he has to be kennelled or left alone for periods, make sure he is well-exercised and stimulated beforehand, so that he is content to rest rather than pick up bad habits through boredom.

MY DOG EATS STONES

Causes: Usually a learned behaviour (playing with stones leading to swallowing them); sometimes due to dietary deficiency; heavy intestinal worm infection (making the dog feel hungry enough to eat anything); pancreatic insufficiency.

Action: If a medical health check finds nothing wrong, it is important to school the dog out of this habit, as eating stones often leads to intestinal blockages, and chewing stones causes dental damage. Work on the 'Drop it' command, using rewards to redirect your dog's attention.

Prevention: Stones make tempting toys for bored dogs, so provide plenty of more suitable toys and games to prevent boredom.

▲ *Puppies naturally tug at clothes in play, but need to learn that fabric is not for chewing.*

MY DOG EATS FABRIC

Causes: Commoner in cats than dogs, fabric-eating is a comfort habit usually caused by stress or boredom; may be linked with too-early weaning.

Action: Helping your dog to relax generally reduces the need for such comfort habits. Try to tackle sources of distress such as separation anxiety, and provide plenty of physical and mental occupation – a dog who has had an interesting day and enough exercise is more likely to spend his spare time sleeping than fretting. Make chewable fabrics as inaccessible as possible, even if you have to put temporary plastic covers on armchairs and hook curtains back out of the way. Dog-owners with teenage children will find this canine problem has its up-side – a couple of chewed-up garments will teach youngsters to put their clothes away!

Prevention: Dogs who feel secure rarely indulge in chewing fabric.

◀ *Take toys to the beach so that your dog doesn't amuse himself with potentially dangerous stones.*

FOOD FOUL-UPS

MY DOG WON'T EAT HIS DINNER

Causes: Learned behaviour (often unintentionally encouraged by owner); too many nibbles between meals; dental problems; neck injury; gastrointestinal disorders; disturbances at feeding site; genuinely unpalatable food.

Action: Check for any physical reason why your dog is not eating. Dental troubles may make eating painful; tall dogs and dogs with neck injuries may find it uncomfortable to reach down for meals, in which case a raised bowl helps. Beyond that, don't make a drama out of dinner! Fussing and coaxing your dog to eat his meal rewards his reluctance. Put his morning meal down, leave him to it, then remove the bowl after 15 minutes whether he has eaten or not. Don't offer any food (including titbits) until you repeat the routine with his next meal, when he will be hungrier. Reducing availability and fuss is often all that is needed.

However, it's also advisable to ensure that your dog can eat in peace without distractions or disturbance. Serve his food in a quiet room. If his collar-tag clinks noisily against his bowl, remove the collar before feeding. Plastic bowls may retain the smell of stale food or detergent, so switching to a metal or ceramic bowl may make meals more appealing. Finally, reluctant eaters need appetising food. Don't fall for the 'I only eat best steak' line, which won't supply all your dog's nutritional needs, but do try different types and textures of food. Moistening dry kibble with a little gravy, or slightly warming food (a few seconds in the microwave) to bring out the smell, often makes dinner more appealing.

Prevention: Establish regular mealtimes (twice a day, morning and evening, suits most dogs) and stick to them. Never reward your dog for refusing a meal by fussing about it or offering tastier alternatives: just remember he will be hungrier next mealtime. However, persistent non-appetite should be checked out with the vet.

MY DOG PREFERS THE CAT'S FOOD TO HIS OWN

Causes: Strong-smelling catfood appeals to many dogs; and there may also be an element of showing the cat who is boss!

Action: The quick-fix solution is to feed the cat in a separate room (perhaps temporarily excluding the dog with a nursery gate) or on a high surface such as a shelf. Teaching the dog that this foodbowl on the floor is his, and that one is the cat's and not to be approached, is a time-consuming task and often hard on the cat. Most cats are leisurely feeders who want to eat in peace, and will be put off by competition. Don't give in to your dog's claim that catfood is tastier. Owners of cat-sized toy breeds sometimes make

▲ Feeding pets too close together is likely to tempt them to investigate each other's dinner.

this mistake, but dogs and cats have different nutritional needs, and a diet of catfood is likely to lead to health problems in dogs.

Prevention: Never allow your dog access to the cat's bowl.

MY DOG INSISTS ON BEING HAND-FED

Causes: If your dog is clearly hungry but reluctant to take food from his bowl, he may have a neck injury. If there is no medical problem, you simply have a dog who has trained you to wait on him.

Action: Try raising your dog's bowl for easier access. If this works, head for the vet to treat neck pain. If your dog is merely being fussy, don't give in! Treat as the faddy feeder (*above*) and insist that your dog feeds himself from his bowl. If the habit is well-established and he is a stubborn creature, he may miss a meal or two while he is learning this lesson, but he is not going to starve himself to death for a principle. Increasing his exercise will help to make him more eager for his dinner.

Prevention: Don't start this practice. A normal healthy dog can feed himself, and it is rarely good for dogs to be babied. A sick dog who cannot leave his bed may need to be hand-fed during his illness, but get him back to his bowl as soon as he can totter over to it, using extra-tempting food (pilchards or cheese are favourites with most dogs) to encourage him if necessary.

◀ *Hand-feeding meals (as opposed to titbits) is inappropriate for a normal healthy dog.*
▼ *Raising the height of his foodbowl often makes eating easier for a stiff or elderly dog.*

Titbits can be fed by hand.

A foodbowl stand can be bought or home-made.

FOOD FOUL-UPS

MY DOG GUARDS HIS DINNER

Causes: Innate food-guarding drive, inappropriately displayed; previous bad experience with meals.

Action: You need to switch your dog's mind-set from 'People might take my food' to 'People give me food'. Next mealtime, put down an empty bowl, then stroll past casually and drop a portion of food into it. Repeat when he has eaten that portion, until the whole meal has been eaten. (If your dog is very aggressive over his bowl, you may need to start by tossing the food into his bowl from a few feet away.) Then simply ignore the bowl, removing it later when the dog is not in the room. Over time, your dog will develop good associations with people approaching his foodbowl, and, once you can feed him normally, you can reinforce these by strolling past to drop an extra-tasty titbit on top of his dinner while he is eating.

Prevention: Make sure your dog has a quiet place for his meals and does not feel under threat while eating. Always ensure that small children are not allowed near the dog's foodbowl at mealtimes.

MY DOG WON'T LET ME TAKE FOOD AWAY FROM HIM

Causes: Innate food-guarding drive, inappropriately displayed; previous bad experience with meals. Owners sometimes create this problem directly

▼ Food-guarding needs to be tackled early on, as this is a potentially dangerous problem. A dog who distrusts people near his food may well bite.

by insisting on taking food away from a dog 'to establish dominance' – a habit more likely to establish distrust.

Action: There are few situations when you need to interrupt a dog's legitimate meal, so don't do it. However, it pays to teach your dog to trust you near his foodbowl, so the practice of occasionally dropping extra titbits into the bowl while he is eating (*see above*) is worth instituting from the start. Teaching your dog to relinquish objects (edible or otherwise) that he has picked up is always worthwhile, so work on the 'Leave it' command, initially with non-food objects until your dog is happy with the exercise, and reward co-operation with favourite titbits. Force rarely works!

Prevention: Respect your dog's mealtimes and only approach his bowl to add to it.

MY DOG SNATCHES TITBITS

Causes: Greed; insecurity (especially if dog has been teased with food in the past); bad manners.
Action: Teach your dog to take food gently by tucking a titbit into your closed hand with just a little bit sticking out, and presenting your hand to him knuckles forward. He will have to sniff around the hand to locate the titbit, and with only a small bit to take hold of, he will have to take it delicately with his lips or front teeth. Rebuke attempts to snatch with a sharp 'No', and praise him when he works out how to take the food carefully. Introducing a command such as 'Gently' will help you to extend this behaviour into other areas.
Prevention: Puppies need to be taught as early as possible to take food gently from fingers. Never punish your puppy for getting it wrong, but withdraw your hand if he snatches, giving an exaggerated squeal of pain to get the message across that fingers are easily hurt, and try again ten minutes later. Never allow children or visitors to tease your dog with titbits.

Extended fingers are vulnerable to an accidental nip.

MY DOG IS AGGRESSIVE OVER BONES

Cause: To a dog, a bone is a valuable asset, and some individuals can become very possessive about them.
Action: If this is a major problem, stop giving your dog bones. Alternatives, such as pigs' ears, will satisfy his gnawing needs, and can be completely consumed in one good chewing session so that there is nothing left over to guard. If your dog merely grumbles when people approach his bone, establish a private corner where he can enjoy his bone in peace, and ensure that all family members respect his privacy. It may help to set up a regular pattern whereby, after he has had a reasonable amount of time with his bone, he is called for a walk or other treat, so that the bone can be removed in his absence.

Children should be taught how to offer food safely to a dog.

Prevention: Teaching basic good manners from puppyhood, including the 'Leave it' command, will discourage this attitude from developing.

◀ *The wrong way to offer titbits! Offering food from above encourages snatching; until your dog has learned manners, keep your hand at his level.*

FOOD FOUL-UPS

MY DOG EATS TOO FAST AND CHOKES

Causes: Greed; fear of losing the food, often arising from bad previous experience (especially in rescue dogs who have been starved).

Action: To slow down the pace at which your dog eats, try placing an empty smaller bowl, or even a suitably sized rock, in the centre of the food bowl, with the food arranged round it.

▶ *If he has to work his way around a rock to get his food, your dog will have to eat more slowly.*

This means your dog has to work round the centrepiece to eat his dinner, instead of gobbling it all in one go. Sometimes using a raised foodbowl is enough to discourage a dog from hoovering up his dinner in one gulp. With hard cases, you may need to hand-feed meals a little at a time. If your dog chokes on his dinner regularly, do check with the vet whether there is some medical reason.

Prevention: Ensure that your dog can eat undisturbed in a quiet place, so that he knows he can eat at a leisurely pace.

MY DOG CARRIES FOOD ALL OVER THE HOUSE

Causes: Some dogs do this, and we don't know why. Some carry away bits of food to hide under cushions and in other inconvenient places, clearly driven by the instinct to cache food against future hard times. Others just like to carry each mouthful away from the bowl, eat it, then return for the next portion – perhaps just because they can!

Action: This is a hard habit to break, and sometimes the only answer is simply to ensure that your dog is fed in a closed room with an easy-clean floor, so that at least all the mess is in one area. A change of diet may lead to a change of habits. Some dogs are deterred from carrying food about by a switch to a wetter diet which is harder to transport. Dry kibble can be served spread out over a large baking tray or cooking sheet to slow down eating.

Prevention: Cross your fingers that your new puppy doesn't turn out to be a food-ferrier!

MY DOG GETS FOOD ALL OVER HIS FACE

Cause: Short-muzzled dogs can be messy eaters; shaggy facial fur and long, fringed ears are almost inevitably going to pick up food particles.
Breed notes: Expect this problem with hairy breeds and long-eared dogs, especially spaniels.

▲ Dogs who swallow grass whole, without chewing it, are more likely to be sick – but don't worry!

▲ Spaniel ears can pick up a horrible amount of dinner – use a deep, narrow bowl so that the ears fall outside it while your dog is eating.

Action: Face-washing after meals needs to become a regular ritual, sponging ear fringes, whiskers, etc. clean with warm water immediately after the meal. Deep foodbowls with narrow openings are specially made for long-eared dogs to keep their ears out of their dinner. Alternatively, you can tie the ears back at mealtimes – you can buy a specially designed ear snood for this purpose, or use a scrap of ribbon. Don't forget to untie them afterwards!
Prevention: Serve a good-quality dry kibble rather than wet food. Even then, dedicated messy dogs will manage to dribble round their whiskers and need a face-wash after dinner.

MY DOG EATS GRASS AND IS THEN SICK

Causes: Most dogs eat grass sometimes, some obsessively, and nobody really knows why. They may feel the need for more greens in their diet, but it is also thought that dogs who feel nauseous seek out grass to ease their stomachs.
Action: Eating grass is a natural action and in most cases you can leave your dog to get on with it, but if he is gobbling large amounts of grass at every opportunity, he may have a digestive disorder. Check that his worm treatment is up to date and consider changing to a higher-fibre diet. You can also try adding steamed, chopped or liquidised greens, such as broccoli, to his dinner. Do watch out to ensure he is not eating grass in areas which have been treated with herbicides or other chemicals.
Prevention: Unless this becomes an obsession, prevention is unnecessary, and you need not prevent your dog from supplementing his diet in this fashion.

FOOD FOUL-UPS

HOW DO I TELL IF MY DOG IS TOO FAT OR TOO THIN?

As a starting point, you should be able to see (and feel) the outline of your dog's ribs. If the ribs are not detectable, he is overweight; if they stick out like a toast rack, he is too thin. Viewed from above, the fit dog has a perceptible waist; viewed from the side, his belly is tucked up higher than his rib-cage. You have to make allowances for body shape in different breeds. At one extreme, Greyhound types are noticeably 'ribby' and have a pronounced 'tuck-up' with deep chest and narrow waist; at the other, chunky dogs like Pugs have more cover over their ribs and minimal waist, but the broad guideline still applies. With long-coated breeds, the body shape may be completely hidden under hair, so your fingers have to do the work, feeling for the ribs and checking for a pendulous, flabby abdomen. You can also get a good idea of your dog's condition at bath-time when the wet hair clings to the body and the underlying shape is revealed.

▲ Real obesity is obvious to the eye without the need for scales or a tape-measure.

HOW DO I KNOW IF MY DOG IS GETTING A BALANCED DIET?

Today we have access to a huge range of commercial dog-foods in canned, semi-moist and kibble form, including special types for different

▲ Regular exercise is as important as diet to keep your dog in sound physical health.

ages, breed types and activity levels, as well as vegetarian and low-calorie meals. Some people prefer to cook fresh food for their dogs; and some consider none of these options as healthy as a 'natural' diet of bones and raw food (known by its initials as the 'BARF' diet). With all this choice, how does an owner decide?

Fortunately, dogs are omnivores who can thrive on a wide variety of diets. Until post-war years, most were fed on household scraps, and did pretty well on them. Most commercially prepared diets and well-planned home-made diets will suit most dogs, unless your pet has special needs or a medical condition, such as gluten allergy. If your dog is active and lively, his digestion is good and his coat is healthy, you can be confident that he is enjoying a balanced diet. If the food you are providing is inappropriate, your dog will provide cues such as loose or foul-smelling stools or constipation, bad breath, a dull or scurfy coat, intestinal gurglings and flatulence, which indicate the need for a review.

Action: When choosing a diet for your dog, bear in mind his age and lifestyle. Specially-formulated puppy food is essential for puppies, who need extra nutrients to support growth and won't thrive on a diet designed for adults, while elderly dogs benefit from a lower-calorie, easily digestible diet. High-protein diets are appropriate for active working dogs, and couch potatoes need fewer calories and less protein.

HOW DO I HELP MY FAT DOG LOSE WEIGHT?

Action: Just like people, dogs lose weight by reducing calorie intake and increasing exercise – but it's a good idea to have a veterinary check-up first. Your vet will be able to recommend a realistic weekly weight loss target and tell you how much food your dog should have each day to achieve this. You can either reduce the amount you feed, or switch to a low-calorie prescription diet. Don't forget to include treats or training reward titbits when measuring the daily ration. Your dog will find his slimming regime easier if you feed little and often, dividing the day's allowance into three or four smaller meals. Cutting out treats altogether may upset him, but you can substitute morsels from his daily ration or low-calorie titbits like raw carrot slices.

▲ *If your dog enjoys swimming, it's one of the best forms of exercise, but remember that not all breeds are natural swimmers.*

▶ *Dogs on a diet don't have to miss out on titbits – try raw carrot chunks or slices for a crunchy, low-calorie treat.*

Make sure your family and friends don't slip him any extras and, if you have other pets, feed them separately to avoid any opportunity for food stealing. Build up exercise (both walks and play-time) gradually. Remember that elderly, unfit or physically immature dogs should not be over-exercised – your vet can give guidance on a realistic programme – and don't push your dog if he shows signs of fatigue. Swimming is a great form of exercise, especially for obese dogs, as it puts less stress on joints than walking. Weigh your dog every fortnight to make sure he is losing weight at a suitable rate – slowly but steadily.

STINKY SITUATIONS

Dogs smell. They are designed to do so – it's an important part of communication between dogs, and a dog that doesn't smell like a dog won't have many canine friends. Most clean, healthy dogs don't offend the human nose, but a pet with a pong can be a problem.

MY DOG'S COAT SMELLS BAD

Causes: Poor hygiene; skin disorder (e.g. seborrhea – a skin condition caused by abnormal secretions of the sebaceous glands); temporary stink from rolling in something horrible; blocked anal glands. Many dogs smell more strongly in old age, especially long-coated breeds.

Breed notes: Hound breeds usually have a characteristic strong 'houndy' smell. Among other breeds, smells adhere more to long or wiry coats than to short coats – so an Otterhound, for example, combining houndy smell and shaggy coat, would be a poor choice for the smell-conscious. Water-loving breeds like Labradors

▲ *Dogs who love swimming in lakes and rivers often need a quick shower when they get home.*

can pick up a wonderful range of stinks from leaping into mucky water at every opportunity.

Action: If your dog smells bad because you haven't been grooming him, the cure is obvious. Incorporating a good quality coat spray designed for your dog's particular type of coat into grooming sessions will further reduce his natural smell. Check his anal glands at the same time, or ask your vet to do it if you are not sure of what to do (*see next entry*). Blocked anal glands not only stink but, if neglected, cause painful abscesses. When tackling a dog who has rolled in disgusting substances, apply tomato juice to neutralise the smell before bathing him very, very thoroughly. If your dog is well-groomed and his anal glands clear, but he still stinks, this suggests a skin problem, which may be treatable by a special shampoo available from your vet.

Prevention: Regular appropriate grooming/ bathing, including attention to anal glands. With intransigently smelly dogs, the regular use of coat sprays is recommended.

MY DOG'S BOTTOM SMELLS

Causes: Faecal soiling; impacted/infected anal glands.

Action: Long-coated dogs quite often suffer from minor or major soiling of the fur under the tail. If they have heavy feathering, this may not be immediately apparent, so it pays to check. Most

commonly, however, the problem is caused by the scent glands beside the anus, which are designed to deposit the dog's scent when he defecates. Modern canine diets don't always contain enough roughage to produce substantial faeces, which means the anal glands may not empty naturally and can become blocked. This causes discomfort (watch for your dog scooting his bottom along the floor) or painful infection, and also produces a foul smell. Ask your vet to check the anal glands, and to empty them if necessary. Changing to a bulkier diet with more fibre, or a raw food diet, may reduce the risk of recurring anal gland problems.

Prevention: Make sure your dog has enough roughage with his meals, and keep an eye on his daily hygiene.

▲ *Bottom-scooting is usually an indication of blocked anal glands – pay a visit to your vet.*

MY DOG'S BREATH SMELLS BAD

Causes: Dental/periodontal problems; digestive problems; anal gland problems.
Breed notes: 'Soft-mouthed' breeds with loose lips (e.g. Cocker Spaniels) can get smelly lip infections if impacted food collects in lip folds.
Action: Inspect teeth – if they are laden with tartar or the gums are red and sore, book a dental session with your vet. If teeth and gums look clean and healthy, bad breath may be caused by digestive problems, in which case a change of diet may improve matters. Charcoal biscuits may also help to improve digestion and clear up bad breath. Anal gland problems can also cause bad breath, as affected dogs transfer the smell from one end to the other when they lick and nibble at the anal irritation.

Prevention: Teach your dog to accept regular mouth inspections. Cleaning teeth regularly with doggy toothpaste prevents build-up of plaque and tartar. A soft, sloppy diet may cause dental problems, so provide your dog with suitable chews (bones, rawhide, raw carrots, good-quality kibble etc.) to clean his teeth naturally. Raw bones and chicken necks are also good for teeth, but are not recommended for toy breeds, and some vets consider this a dangerous diet anyway because of the risk of splinters. Breath-freshening products simply mask any problem rather than curing it.

▶ *Neglected, tartar-laden teeth can cause health problems as well as foul breath.*
▼ *Prevent the build-up of tartar by cleaning with a finger-mounted toothbrush.*

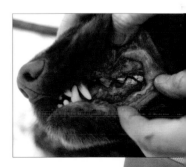

STINKY SITUATIONS

MY DOG'S EARS SMELL BAD

Causes: Bacterial infection; mite infestation; allergy; foreign body (e.g. grass seed); excess wax; excess ear hair.

Breed notes: Floppy-eared breeds (e.g. spaniels) are at risk of ear problems because reduced air circulation in the ear canals creates an ideal environment for bacteria, mites, etc. Very hairy breeds (e.g. Lhasa Apso) may have similar problems because of excess ear hair.

Action: See the vet immediately. Healthy ears smell clean: stinky ears are unhealthy, uncomfortable and often painful. Delay in treatment may result in permanently damaged hearing.

Prevention: Check ears regularly: they should look clean and should not smell. Visible wax or dirt can be gently removed with damp cotton wool, but never poke inside the ear canal, which tends to push dirt or foreign bodies further in. You may need to trim or pluck hair inside the ears to allow air to circulate – if necessary, ask your dog's breeder or a professional groomer to show you how to do this painlessly. Heavy ears (spaniel type) can be tied back occasionally for the same reason. Diet may be a factor in ear problems – excess carbohydrate can encourage yeast infections – so discuss alternative diets with your vet.

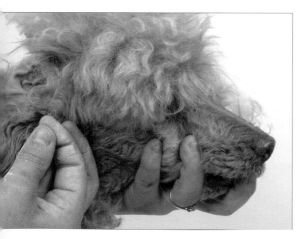

▲ Removing excessive hair from inside the ears must be done gently and with care. Heavy-handed plucking can lead to irritation and infection.

MY DOG KEEPS BREAKING WIND

Causes: Unsuitable diet/overfeeding; eating too fast and swallowing air; breed tendency; insufficient exercise; symptom of digestive disorders such as pancreatic insufficiency.

Breed notes: Certain breeds are notoriously flatulent. Boxers are the acknowledged champions in this respect, but Labradors and Rottweilers are also on the list.

Action: A change of diet may solve the problem: try a gradual switch to a higher-quality dog food based on chicken or lamb, avoiding brands with a high cereal content, and cut out table scraps. Adding a spoonful of live yoghurt to your dog's meal may help to improve digestion and reduce gas – though dogs who are lactose intolerant will be less gassy if they avoid all dairy products. Charcoal helps to detoxify noxious gases, so adding a little activated charcoal to your dog's meal reduces nasty smells, but beware: it also reduces your dog's nutrient intake from his food, so should never be used more than once or twice a week. Dogs who bolt their food need to be helped to slow down (*see p.18*). Simply increasing

◀ ▲ *Remote-control collars are best introduced with professional guidance.*

harmless but strong-smelling citronella spray when activated, so that the moment he heads for temptation he experiences an unpleasant sensation. This is harder than it sounds, as you have catch your dog in the act to time the deterrent appropriately. Squirting him at the wrong moment will simply confuse him. In areas where smelly temptations are most likely to be found, keeping your dog on the leash may be the best solution. If your dog tends to roll immediately after a bath, it may be that he is attempting to mask the smell of the shampoo, and switching to a different shampoo can help.

Prevention: Keeping your dog's attention on you during walks reduces the likelihood of his discovering temptation in the first place.

your dog's amount of exercise to an appropriate level may solve the problem by improving his digestion. Chronic flatulence which does not respond to any of the above should be checked out by the vet, especially if linked with any other symptoms of poor condition, as it may indicate an underlying digestive problem requiring treatment. However, some individuals seem to be persistently flatulent whatever you do, and you may just have to learn to live with this.

Prevention: Establish a healthy regime of exercise and well-balanced diet.

MY DOG ROLLS IN SMELLY SUBSTANCES

Cause: Dogs enjoy many smells that we don't appreciate, and some just love to wallow in them.

Action: With persistent rollers, eternal vigilance is the first step — try to spot tempting objects like dead fish or piles of dung before your dog does, so that you can leash him or recall him. Next, you need to introduce a deterrent such as a water pistol or a remote-control collar which blasts him with

▲ *Most dogs love to roll, often in scents too faint for us to notice. Unfortunately, some dogs are also good at finding really stinky things to roll in.*

STINKY SITUATIONS

MY DOG SMELLS OF URINE

Causes: Long-haired dogs may soil their underparts when urinating; some males never learn to aim properly and widdle on their own feet; urine leakage may be caused by medical conditions such as cystitis, bladder problems, kidney failure or diabetes, and also is not uncommon in spayed bitches and older animals.

Action: Start with a veterinary check-up to exclude medical conditions. If your vet gives the all-clear, turn to ways of improving your dog's hygiene. With long-haired dogs, trim the fur on

▶ *Puddles need to be deodorised as well as mopped, or a smell can build up. Tackle them with enzyme-based cleaners.*

the undercarriage. You may also need to clip any leg feathering. With young dogs who spray their own paws when cocking a leg, maturity may solve the situation as they learn to cock their legs higher, but with some individuals this is a lifetime problem. Wiping down legs and paws after every outing with warm water with a little vinegar added to it, or with a mild shampoo, may be necessary to keep your dog comfortable and unsmelly.

Prevention: Maintain good coat hygiene, and seek veterinary help if appropriate.

MY HOUSE SMELLS OF URINE

Cause: During house-training, indoor accidents will happen, and sometimes the smell lingers on.

Action: When mopping up puddles, use an enzyme-based cleaner specifically designed to tackle canine urine. Ordinary household cleaners rarely remove the odour completely. Carpets in particular hold smells, and you may need to use a steam-cleaner to get right down to the underlay. Do check in dark corners and behind furniture, where the odd little puddle may escape attention to soak in and leave a lingering smell – tiny toy breed puppies in particular tend to leave tiny puddles which may not be noticed until the carpet has become pongy.

Prevention: While working on house-training, it pays to limit your dog's unsupervised access to carpeted areas. If you have to go out and leave him alone, restricting him to a room with a wipe-down floor such as the kitchen, or teaching him to accept a crate, makes it easier to keep down smells.

MY GARDEN SMELLS OF DOG MESS

Cause: Owner's failure to clear up after dog.
Action: Clear up canine faeces morning and evening on a regular basis. You may wish to instal a 'doggy loo', which can be bought from specialist pet stores or web-based suppliers. This is a mini-septic tank where you deposit your dog's waste and it is biologically treated by the addition of a special solution and then dispersed harmlessly into the soil. Alternatively, you can just 'bag it and bin it' – never put dog waste on the compost heap, as it won't make good compost and may be a health hazard.

Cleaning up is easier if you train your dog to use a specific toileting area in the garden with a suitable surface such as mulch or pea gravel (and, for males, some form of marking post – anything from a large rock to a garden gnome!). Take your dog there on a leash for toilet breaks, rewarding him when he uses the right place until he learns the purpose of this zone. You can speed up the training process by 'salting' the designated area with your dog's most recent offering.

Prevention: Monitor your dog's toilet habits from day one, and be punctilious about cleaning up.

◀ *Pick up poop straight away as a hygiene measure.*

MY PATIO SMELLS OF URINE

Cause: Hard surfaces such as concrete, stone, etc. soak up smells, and if a dog urinates repeatedly in such areas, the smell of old urine can become very strong.
Action: Wash the area thoroughly using a specially

◀ *During house-training, set aside a cheap mop and cleaning rags specifically for cleaning up doggy accidents, and disinfect them well after use.*

designed pet odour eliminator, available from most pet shops – household cleaners are not designed for this job, and will not eradicate the smell totally. If the problem has built up over a long time, you will need to really soak the concrete and not just go over the surface.
Prevention: Teach your dog to regard the patio as part of the house and do not allow him to urinate there. Initially this will mean never allowing him unsupervised access, so that you are always to hand to correct any mistakes, but most dogs will soon learn the rules. If accidents happen, wash down any suspiciously wet areas with diluted bleach as soon as you spot them.

▲ *Concrete patios and edging retain urine smells, so wash them down regularly if your dog is cocking his leg on these areas of the garden.*

STINKY SITUATIONS

MY HOUSE SMELLS OF WET DOG

Cause: Wet dog! Many dog breeds have the type of coat that takes on a strong odour when wet, and the smell tends to linger throughout the house.

Action: Drying your soggy dog with towels after every wet walk will still leave his fur damp enough to smell, and the only way to eradicate the pong is to complete the job thoroughly with a hairdryer. (You can save time and effort by buying or making a towelling dog-drying bag, which encloses your dog from the neck downwards and absorbs the worst of the wet very quickly.) Not many people have the time and patience to carry out a full grooming session every time their pet goes out in the rain, and if you have a shaggy-coated breed the 'wet dog' odour may well have more endurance than you have. In this case, air fresheners may be the only answer, although regular applications of a fragranced grooming spray when you are brushing your dog will reduce the problem. Although

▶ *Towel-drying may be enough if your dog has just popped out in a light shower, but if he's very wet he needs more.*

towelling won't remove the smell, it's still important to rub your dog down after a swim or a walk in the rain. Never leave a wet dog to dry naturally: quite apart from the smell, the damp is not good for his joints and may lead to arthritis.

Prevention: Choosing a smooth-coated breed with no interest in swimming, such as a Pug, reduces the risk of 'wet dog' smell. If you have already given your heart to a dog with a naturally strong-smelling, shaggy coat, such as an Otterhound, you are unlikely to be able to prevent the problem and will need to bring out the air-fresheners.

MY HOUSE SMELLS 'DOGGY'

Causes: Naturally strong-smelling breed; carpets and soft furnishings retaining canine smell; inadequate grooming. Multiple dog ownership increases the likelihood of this problem!

Action: Daily grooming and a monthly bath with a good-quality canine shampoo will keep your dog's natural smell to a minimum, and a regular household cleaning routine will reduce its impact. Air rooms frequently, and wash your dog's bedding material on a regular basis – a washable dog bed that can be popped into the washing machine is a good investment if you have a noticeably odoriferous pet. Areas where your dog spends time – not just his bed but favourite sites such as the corner in the hall where he lies to watch the front door – retain doggy smells and require extra cleaning.

◀ Watch out – wet dogs love to spread a coat-load of water via a good shake.

build up in a house, and by the time it has become a problem the dog-owner can easily grow so accustomed to it as to fail to notice it. To prevent reaching this stage, ask non-doggy friends for their opinion from time to time! With the more manageable breeds, a regular routine of grooming and housework will keep your house smelling fresh. With smellier breeds, or if you keep a pack rather than a single pet, more grooming and more housework are necessary and you will probably have to think in terms of managing the problem rather than preventing it altogether.

Carpets, cushions (and chairs, if your dog is allowed on the furniture) will benefit from shampooing or steam cleaning – or, for a quick fix, try sprinkling a little bicarbonate of soda on to a stinky carpet and leave it for a few hours to absorb the smell before vacuuming it up. If the problem is getting you down, consider replacing carpets with wipe-down vinyl flooring and having washable covers on furniture.

Any lingering aroma can be masked with air fresheners or, if you prefer, by hanging up bunches of scented herbs, such as lavender *(left)* and rosemary. Herbs also come in useful when planted densely by the door where your dog will brush against them as he comes in, picking up the fragrance on his coat – scented geraniums are particularly effective here.

Prevention: It takes time for the 'doggy' smell to

▲ How often you need to bath your dog depends on his coat type and personal habits – some dogs stay sweet-smelling with only an occasional bath.

MESSY MATTERS

Caring for living creatures, from hamsters to babies, has its messy side, as dog owners often find. House-training doesn't always go as smoothly as expected, mud and moult can turn a home into a hovel, and cleaning can be a chore.

▶ *Constant vigilance is needed to catch your puppy before he wees.*

MY DOG URINATES/DEFECATES INDOORS

Causes: Medical problems, e.g. cystitis, diabetes; dog left indoors without sufficient provision for toileting outside; stress; territorial/status display; age; failure of house-training. Age is an obvious factor: puppies and many elderly dogs have reduced bladder and bowel control, while adolescents may be 'high' on hormones and want to make their mark – like human teenagers pinning up posters or spraying graffiti. If a previously clean dog starts to toilet indoors, the likely cause is stress (often caused by separation anxiety or by changes in the household).

Action: First check that there is no medical reason for the puddles, and also that your dog has adequate opportunities to empty his bladder outside. If all is well on both counts, set aside a week or two for an intensive house-training programme when you can be on hand to supervise him full-time. If you have to leave him for short periods (not more than an hour at a time), confine him in a comfortable safe area, such as a crate or a corner of the kitchen. Throughout the day, take him out for a toilet break every hour, letting him potter about and sniff for five minutes or so. Don't pressure him to perform, but praise him if he does take the opportunity. Times when he is most likely to urinate or defecate are just after waking up, after eating, after a play session and, of course, after demonstrating such indicators as sniffing, circling round, looking uncomfortable or beginning to squat. If accidents do happen indoors, never scold or punish him, which may well make him fearful of toileting in your presence even in approved areas. It may also lead him to start defecating in concealed spots, such as behind the sofa, or even eating the evidence. It is better, therefore, to ignore him and get on with cleaning up quietly. Be sure to use an ammonia-free cleaner designed for the purpose: ordinary household cleaners will leave smell traces detectable to a dog's nose which will encourage him to urinate in that spot again.

▶ *A crate can be a useful house-training aid, but only if supported by frequent toilet breaks outside in the garden.*

Prevention: Spend time on house-training from day one, whether you have a baby puppy or an adult rescue dog.

MY DOG ISN'T CLEAN AT NIGHT

Causes: Medical problems, e.g. cystitis, diabetes; age (like small children and old people, puppies and elderly dogs often can't last out the whole night); stress/insecurity; failure to extend house-training into the night period.

Action: A medical check is the first step. With puppies and ageing dogs, you may need to make provision for weak bladders by bedding your dog down for the night in a confined area with an easy-clean surface. If he is neither ill, old nor a

or two of interrupted sleep, but most dogs will adapt to your own habits and start sleeping through the night.

With dogs who are anxious left on their own, an owner's reassuring presence may be enough to resolve the problem. If you prefer your dog to sleep elsewhere, you can make the move in gradual stages once he has established the habit of being clean at night.

▲ After your puppy has had a sleep, he will need to wee, so rush him outside when he wakes up.

puppy, make sure he has a good long walk before bedtime with plenty of toilet opportunities and move him into your own bedroom at night, confining him to a bed in a crate. Most dogs won't wet their own beds, so you should be alerted by sounds of fidgeting when he needs a toilet break. (Try putting a bell on his collar if you are a heavy sleeper.) At such times, slip on his lead and take him out into the garden for five minutes. Don't make a fuss about this (you don't want it to seem either a treat or a punishment, just a routine procedure), but praise him if he performs, and then take him back to bed. It will cost you a week

▲ Schedule frequent toileting opportunities in the garden. If you don't have a garden, frequent short trips out are preferable to paper-training.

MESSY MATTERS

MY DOG WEES WHEN GREETING PEOPLE

Cause: Submissive behaviour – the canine way of showing extreme respect. This is a common behaviour in young puppies; in adults, it shows insecurity (usually arising from inadequate socialisation or mistreatment; sometimes from an innate overly submissive nature) and should not be regarded as a failure of house-training.

Action: Don't scold your dog, or he will feel the need to demonstrate even more submissiveness and the problem will worsen. Don't reassure him, or you will be rewarding him for weeing. Simply ignore what has happened and keep calm. Avoid excited greetings: when you come home, say hello in passing and defer contact for five minutes while you potter about ignoring him, then crouch, kneel or sit before calling him for a fuss. It is important to avoid dominant body language, which is why you need to crouch down to greet your dog rather than looming over him, and you should also avoid direct eye

▶ *Crouching down rather than looming over a dog is less likely to elicit an over-submissive response and the dog wetting himself.*

contact, do not pick him up, and pet him under the chin or on the chest rather than reaching down to stroke his back or the top of the head. Ask guests to treat him in the same way. You can also build up your dog's confidence through reward-based training, teaching him alternative ways to greet you such as offering a paw, and through play – encouraging him to win at games of tug of war will help him to feel bolder.

Prevention: Ensure that puppies are well socialised, and avoid choosing the shyest pup in the litter.

MY DOG COCKS HIS LEG ON FURNITURE

Cause: Territorial marking, typically by young entire males, but occasionally in castrated males and females. This is usually caused by competition for status, either in a multi-dog household or where a single dog is not clear about his status in the human family hierarchy; it can also be triggered by visitors. Once a dog has marked a spot, he is likely to be drawn back to the same area to update his mark.

Action: Clean soiled areas with an ammonia-free cleaner to remove the cue to repeat the behaviour. Keep your dog under close supervision for a couple of weeks –

◄ Make sure your dog knows where he can cock his leg and where he shouldn't do so.

confine him to one area of the house where you can watch him, or keep him attached to you on an extending lead. If you can catch him in the act, scold him with a sharp 'No', and hurry him outside, praising him if he cocks his leg in the appropriate area. Increasing time spent on fun, reward-based training, teaching your dog any exercises from a simple 'Sit' to complicated 'heelwork to music' routines, will help to establish his rank in the household as being below yours and therefore make it clear to him that it is not his place to mark territory. Where possible, avoid having canine visitors, as this will stimulate territorial marking. In a multi-dog household, castrating the lower-ranking dog may resolve this problem; however, although neutering reduces the urge to mark territory, it is unlikely to halt the behaviour once it has been learned and you will still need to work on re-training. If you are considering neutering as a cure, it may be worth trying chemical castration (a temporary measure) to see if it helps.

Prevention: Neutering at an early age usually prevents the habit from forming; otherwise, spend time on supervision as soon as your dog is old enough to cock his leg.

MY DOG LEAKS URINE WHEN ASLEEP

Cause: A range of medical conditions including weak bladder sphincter; hormonal problems; urinary tract infection; or an ailment producing an abnormal amount of urine, such as diabetes.

The problem is commonest in older bitches and may be linked to early spaying.

Action: See your vet immediately to establish the cause of the problem. Most cases will respond to the appropriate medication. In the meantime, it is important to keep your dog's underparts clean and dry, washing soiled areas with a mild anti-bacterial soap and drying thoroughly to prevent urine burns to the skin, as well as smelly fur. You may also find it helpful to place waterproofing under your dog's bedding, or to line his bed with a washable rubber-backed bathmat.

◄ ▲ A dog who wets the bed while asleep needs a trip to the vet, who can usually solve the problem.

MESSY MATTERS

MY DOG WEES WHEN VISITING FRIENDS

Causes: A dog can be perfectly house-trained in his own home, but fail to realise that this learned behaviour is expected to apply in other environments such as friends' homes or hotel rooms (especially if there are, or have been, other animals in the place you are visiting). Alternatively, excitement or stress may cause a dog to pass a little urine when visiting.

Action: Make sure your dog has toileting opportunities before entering your friends' home. When visiting anywhere for the first time, keep your dog under close supervision just as if you

▲ To you it's a new rug, to be treated with care. To him, it's a new smell that needs weeing on.

were house-training for the first time, watching for any signs that he is about to urinate, when you should tell him 'No' and rush him outside. Don't let him out of your sight until you have visited several times and are sure he has learned the routine. When visiting friends who have dogs of their own (or who have had dogs in the house in the past), take extra care, as the canine smells may stimulate your dog to leave his mark. If he wees just a little because he is excited or nervous, treat as submissive urination (*see p.32*).

Prevention: Once your dog is fully house-trained at home, extend his training to other environments, keeping close watch so that he does not have the opportunity to make mistakes.

MY DOG WEES ON MY NEW RUG

Cause: Territorial marking. New carpets and rugs often contain chemicals which to a dog's sensitive nose smell very like urine, stimulating him to urinate or defecate over the scent.

Action: Always supervise your dog in the presence

▲ When visiting, keep your dog close beside you – don't let him explore and perhaps leave his mark.

of new carpeting or rugs. At the first indicator that he may be about to make his mark, tell him 'No' and rush him outside, encouraging him to perform in the approved area. Over the next few days the carpet will take on the smell of home, and you will be able to relax. With a rug, the simplest approach is to put it down short-term under supervision and take it up whenever you are out of the room. If your dog is a persistent offender, try serving his meals on the new rug, as few dogs will toilet where they eat. Place a shallow plastic tray or place-mat under his dinner bowl to catch any food spillage, stand over him while he eats, and praise him for being on the rug without urinating.

Prevention: Supervise, supervise and supervise!

◥ *Vacuum over the soiled area after thorough cleaning.*

◀ *When your dog visits other dogs, it's natural canine behaviour for him to scent-mark, so be alert.*

HOW DO I TACKLE URINE STAINS ON CARPETS, ETC?

Fresh stains: Rinse with cold water and treat with pet deodoriser. Washable items can be washed as normal, using a biological detergent to remove lingering smells. With carpets, blot up as much liquid as possible with an old towel and sponge the stain with salt water, then with clear, before blotting dry again. Remember to soak right down to the underfelt for thorough cleaning. To remove trace smells that may draw your dog back to the site, sprinkle bicarbonate of soda over the soiled area and leave it to dry before vacuuming thoroughly.

Dried stains: Washable fabrics should be soaked overnight in salt water before being washed as above. For carpets, you can buy stain removers containing enzyme inhibitors designed to tackle pet urine, or you can mix your own (always testing on an obscure corner to check that it will not bleach the colour). Try scrubbing with a mixture of white vinegar, washing-up liquid and water; or white toothpaste and a little warm water; or very diluted hydrogen peroxide (no more than 3% to 97% water). Rinse thoroughly afterwards with warm water. If the stain reappears a few days later, soak with water and repeat the cleaning process. If you have a steam cleaner, this will permeate further into the carpet fabric.

MESSY MATTERS

HOW DO I DEAL WITH POOP IN THE GARDEN?

Action: It makes life simpler if you set aside a designated toilet area in the garden for your dog's sole use, rather than allow him to use the whole garden. Mark out the chosen area, and take your dog there on a leash as soon as he wakes up, after meals, after play and whenever he shows signs of wanting to empty his bowels. Encourage him to perform with a suitable phrase, such as 'Hurry up', and reward him when he does so. While he is learning what this area is for, it may help to leave his most recent deposit there as a scent cue to remind him. Be persistent and consistent, and eventually your time and patience will be rewarded with a dog who heads for the designated area when he wants to toilet.

Whether you choose to take this route or allow your dog the run of the garden, you need to clear up his faeces regularly – say every morning and evening. The simplest approach is to slip a plastic bag over your hand, pick up the mess, turn the bag inside out to enclose the mess as you slip your hand out, and tie the top. You then have a neat package which you can dispose of in any legal container. Alternatively you can instal a 'doggy loo' (*see p.27*), or use an incinerator. Long-handled scooper tools with disposable bags are available for those who find bending difficult. The average dog has some 23 bowel movements per week, so if this task is neglected a garden can quickly become unsavoury and smelly, to say nothing of unhygienic – canine waste may contain a range of disease-transmitting

▶ *Disposable 'poo bags' make picking up poop easier and less messy.*

organisms, from bacteria to roundworms. Picking up will also prevent your dog from developing the unsavoury habit of eating his own faeces, as he may if they are constantly available.

HOW DO I DEAL WITH POOP ON WALKS?

Action: Always be prepared with poop-scoop bags when you go out, even if your dog has already toileted in the garden – accidents can happen. Picking up after your dog is a legal requirement in many areas, and a good habit in general.

HOW DO I REMOVE FAECAL STAINS FROM CARPETS AND SOFT FURNISHINGS?

Action: Start by scraping off as much solid matter as you can – an old spoon is ideal. Washable items, such as cushion covers, should be soaked in cold water for an hour or so before being washed on the hottest cycle possible, using biological detergent. With carpets, soak the soiled area in a solution of biological detergent and warm water to loosen the stain, leave for a while, then scrub with carpet shampoo and rinse with cold water. Really tough stains may require the use of a steam-cleaner. Having tackled the stain, it is also important to remove any lingering odour which may encourage your dog to return to the same

▶ *Dogs, like children, will get upset stomachs from time to time, and mild diarrhoea is no cause for real concern.*

MY DOG HAS DIARRHOEA

Causes: The occasional bout of diarrhoea is nothing to be worried about and can be due to your dog eating the wrong thing, eating too much or too fast, stress, excitement, or strenuous exercise too soon after eating. More serious cases can be caused by anything from food allergy to a life-threatening virus.

Action: If there is blood in the faeces or the condition is accompanied by vomiting, breathing difficulties or signs of pain, see your vet immediately. Otherwise, withhold food for the next 24 hours to allow the dog's intestinal tract time to recover. If the condition persists for more than 24 hours, it is also wise to seek veterinary advice.

Prevention: Feed your dog a sensible balanced diet, provide appropriate worming treatment and maintain vaccination boosters – and expect the occasional mild stomach upset from time to time in any case, because dogs will be dogs! It just makes cleaning up that much harder.

▲ *Discourage your dog from investigating (or eating) other dogs' faeces when out on walks, as these can be a source of stomach upsets.*

spot. Various commercial products are available, or you can simply sprinkle baking soda over the area, leave overnight and then vacuum.

MESSY MATTERS

MY NORMALLY HOUSE-TRAINED DOG MESSES INDOORS WHEN LEFT ALONE

Causes: Inadequate toileting provision; medical problems; separation anxiety.

Action: If you are leaving your dog alone for long periods without access to an appropriate toilet area, the solution is obvious! However, if your dog regularly urinates or defecates indoors when left for short periods, and if you have eliminated medical problems, the most likely cause is separation anxiety. Never punish your dog for making a mess in your absence; it's wasted effort, since the dog will not associate present punishment with the past offence, and also counter-productive, since it is likely to increase his stress levels. Instead, work on building up his confidence when left alone (see pp.148-9). Punctiliously clean and deodorise areas where he has soiled to remove scent cues that will encourage him to repeat the behaviour. You may need to restrict his access to targeted areas while you are out, settling him down in a corner of the kitchen, or in a crate if he is comfortable with this. (If he

▲ Unless you catch him in the act, scolding your dog is counter-productive – just mop up quietly.

does not feel safe and happy in a crate, it will only increase his anxiety). You can also make those areas less appealing for toileting by feeding him there, leaving his water bowl on the spot, or spraying that part of the room with a deterrent spray. It is important to tackle the problem of separation anxiety as a whole rather than focusing on the toileting aspect of it, accustoming your dog to be left for gradually longer periods.

Prevention: From day one, practise leaving your dog for very short periods – one or two minutes to begin with – every day, building up the time in small increments.

MY DOG WON'T TOILET IN THE GARDEN

Cause: House-training confusion – your dog has learned that he should not toilet in certain places, i.e. indoors, and has extended the lesson to include the garden.

▲ Most dogs won't toilet near their food and water bowls, so use these as deterrents.

Action: Start house-training again from scratch, taking your dog out as soon as he wakes up, after meals, and at frequent regular intervals and waiting with him. If possible, 'salt' the chosen area in the garden with his recent faeces or a urine sample, if you can collect one, to provide a scent signal indicating that this is a toilet area; you could also ask a friend to bring their dog into the garden (while your dog waits indoors) to urinate there. You may have to persist for a couple of weeks if your dog is very firmly fixed in his ideas, but it is worth the effort.

Prevention: Successful house-training in the first place means this problem won't occur; but if you take on a dog who is already confused about the subject, you will have to undo someone else's mistakes.

MY DOG HAS A DIRTY BOTTOM

Cause: Soft, sticky motions will adhere to the fur around a dog's anus, and this can be a real problem with long-haired dogs with thick 'breeches'. Diarrhoea will also cause soiling.

Action: Short-term, the task is to clean up. For recent heavy soiling, rinse the area with warm water and then wash with a little canine shampoo, drying thoroughly after the final rinse. Lighter soiling can often be dealt with by sprinkling with talcum powder and combing out. If faecal traces have dried in the fur, the simplest rule is to comb out light soiling and clip out heavy soiling. With dogs who have very dense fur, it is sometimes advisable to clip the area around the anus in any case to prevent fouling. If the problem is recurrent, you should review your dog's diet with a view to producing firmer stools. This can be a matter of trial and error, although bland chicken and rice diets often help.

Prevention: Check your long-haired dog's personal hygiene on at least a daily basis and tackle soiling promptly. Ensure that long fur around the anus is thoroughly combed through, as tangles in this area will make it difficult for your dog to pass a motion and can result in a horrible mess; clip if necessary. Monitor your dog's diet, seeking veterinary guidance if you are unable to find food he can digest properly.

Regular combing keeps on top of tangles.

◀ *Long-haired dogs need to have their breechings and tails checked and combed through at least daily for hygiene's sake.*

MESSY MATTERS

MY DOG WEES ON HIS OWN FORELEGS

Causes: Young males have to learn the skill of cocking a leg accurately, and can often have poor aim at first; most learn with time, but a few never seem quite to get the knack and can soak their own underparts and/or forelegs. Occasionally there is a physical cause for this (minor penile malformations can affect aim), but usually it is simple clumsiness. To a dog, of course, reeking of his own urine is perfectly acceptable and indeed comforting; it is only humans who object!

Action: Clean your dog's legs and underparts after every soggy outing, using warm water or doggy wipes. There is no need to use shampoo if you can clean up before the soiling dries but, if you prefer to do so, it is worth buying a rinseless shampoo, available from most pet stores. This is a spray-on shampoo which can be rubbed into the soiled fur to form a light lather, and then simply blotted dry without the need for rinsing – a great time-saver. Dry shampoos are useful if you don't have access to water, but are messier and leave some residue in the coat. With long-haired dogs, some judicial clipping of leg and belly feathering will reduce the amount of soiling. (Do not clip the tassel on the end of the penis sheath, as this actually helps to direct urine away from the fur.)

▶ *Nobody likes cuddling a dog who has wet himself.*

production, creating the moist environment that encourages these organisms, is generally due to eye shape and structure – breeds with even slightly prominent eyes tend to have this problem – but can also be caused by allergies, eye or ear infections, the pH of your dog's drinking water, blocked tear ducts, ingrowing eyelashes, teething in puppies, and irritation by hair in the eyes.

MY DOG HAS A TEAR-STAINED FACE

Cause: Tear stains around the eyes are caused by bacterial or yeast growth which thrive in moisture – most commonly an organism known as 'red yeast', which causes reddish-brown staining. Excess tear

▶ *With fluffy white breeds like Maltese, tear stains are conspicuous and keeping on top of them requires real commitment.*

▶ ▼ White Boxers are often prone to tear stains — a minor problem that usually responds to warm water.

cosmetic problem. For most pet owners, the best approach is to ask a professional groomer to do their best. Home remedies (usually mixtures of milk of magnesia, corn starch, bleach, lemon juice or peroxide) are best left to experienced handlers to avoid the risk of damaging the eyes. In many cases, the stains can only be lightened, and not removed entirely.

Prevention: With dogs prone to this problem, clean the fur around the eyes several times a day with warm water. You may need to keep the hair around the eyes trimmed, using blunt-ended scissors. Maintain a healthy diet and keep your dog in a clean atmosphere — stale or smoky air can irritate the eyes. When bathing the dog, take extra care to avoid getting shampoo in his eyes.

Note: Similar staining can also occur around the mouth. This is sometimes due to colourants in dog-food, but again is often caused by red yeast or similar organisms and can be tackled as above.

Light-coloured dogs, especially those with shaggy beards, often need to have their muzzles washed and dried after eating and drinking to prevent this problem. Using ceramic food and water bowls (rather than steel or plastic) is also recommended.

Breed notes: Tear stains are most conspicuous on fluffy white dogs, such as Maltese or Bichons, but affect many other breeds, including Bulldogs, Cocker Spaniels and St Bernards.

Action: Ask your vet to ascertain the cause of staining, as treatment may be necessary for infections and severe problems, such as ingrowing eyelashes, require surgery. In some cases your vet may prescribe eye drops to dilate the tear ducts and prevent overflowing. You may be able to reduce tear production by a change of diet or trimming facial hair. Adding a teaspoon of white vinegar to your dog's drinking water will discourage yeast and bacteria. Once you have tackled physical causes, removal of existing stains is a

MESSY MATTERS

MY DOG SCOOTS HIS BOTTOM ALONG THE GROUND

Causes: The commonest cause is blocked or infected anal glands. These glands, situated on either side of the dog's rectum, produce a smelly fluid which is squeezed out when the dog empties his bowels to act as a scent-marker. In domestic dogs, the glands don't always empty properly, with results ranging from discomfort to large abscesses. Your dog may also have a sore or itchy bottom due to tapeworm infestation, soreness after diarrhoea, skin infection or allergies.

Action: See your vet to identify the cause. If the problem is simply blocked anal glands, the vet can empty these manually. The condition is likely to recur; to avoid regular visits to the vet, you can ask him to teach you how to empty the glands yourself. If the glands have become infected, your dog will need antibiotics, and any abscesses will need to be bathed in salt water. If a dog's anal glands cause a lot of problems, a change of diet may help, as low-quality food, insufficient roughage and food intolerance have all been linked with this condition. In severe cases, some vets favour surgical removal of the glands, although many consider this an over-drastic treatment.

Prevention: Maintaining a healthy diet reduces the likelihood of anal gland problems. Check your dog's anal area daily so that any irritation can be caught in the early stages.

▲ If unspayed, bitches generally come into season twice a year (in some breeds, only once).
▼ Never ignore a dog with an itchy bottom!

this lasts about three weeks, during which she will normally produce a bloody vaginal discharge, usually beginning towards the end of the first week of oestrus and continuing for 10-14 days. The amount of discharge varies; some individuals may have a 'silent heat' with no (or hardly any) traces, while others can be quite messy. Most bitches keep themselves clean, but there may be stains on carpets or chairs.

Action: When your bitch is in season, you may wish to confine her to an easily cleaned area or put covers on furniture. Some owners prefer to put their bitch into 'hygiene pants' to protect furnishings from stains. However, bloodstains are usually minimal and easily removed. For fresh stains, scrub with cold water; tackle dried stains with a paste of cornstarch and water, rinse with cold water, blot dry and then vacuum. Diluted hydrogen peroxide is also highly effective on bloodstains.

Prevention: If you do not wish to breed from your bitch, spaying is the obvious solution.

MY FEMALE DOG LEAVES STAINS WHEN SHE IS IN SEASON

Cause: An unspayed bitch comes into season once or twice a year, depending on the breed. In general

MY DOG COMES HOME COVERED IN MUD

Cause: As the proverb says, mud sticks — and long-coated dogs in particular can pick up an astonishing amount of mud on a wet walk.

Action: There are two approaches to tackling muddy dogs, depending on the amount of mud and your degree of house-proudness. The simplest method is to towel-dry the dog, leaving the mud to dry, and brush out the dried mud later on. With a very muddy, long-coated dog this is likely to produce mats and tangles, and it is better to rinse the dog off in the bath before drying – there is no need to use shampoo, just warm water. Mud on carpets and furnishings is usually best left to dry, then brushed off with a soft bristle brush and vacuumed clean. (Scrubbing mud while it is still wet simply pushes it deeper into carpet fibres.) If stains remain after you have brushed off the dried mud, work stain remover into the area and leave for a few minutes

▲ After a muddy walk, your dog needs cleaning up and drying, not just to keep your home clean but also as part of his health maintenance – a dirty, matted coat leads to skin problems.

before rinsing thoroughly and blotting dry.

Prevention: It really is worth spending time teaching your dog to stop at the door when he gets home and wait to have his paws (or the whole of his body if necessary) dried with a towel. With a long-coated dog who is addicted to muddy explorations, a bit of judicious clipping will reduce your workload, trimming the feathering from legs and underparts. If you and your dog enjoy country walks in the rain, you may wish to replace carpets with wipe-down flooring.

MESSY MATTERS

MY DOG MOULTS EVERYWHERE

Causes: Dogs moult throughout the year, with two peaks in spring and autumn when they shed their winter or summer coats, and dogs who live indoors in heated houses moult more frequently. Excessive moulting can be caused by allergies, central heating and warm weather, but is often characteristic of a particular breed.

Breed notes: Long-haired, double-coated dogs (such as Siberian Huskies *(below)* and Pyrenean Mountain Dogs) moult copiously and conspicuously, but many short-haired breeds (such as Dalmatians and Labradors) also shed hairs prolifically – and short hairs are harder to remove from clothes and furniture.

▶ *A slicker brush helps to remove moulted hairs.*

Action: Regular thorough grooming, especially during the moult, reduces the amount of hair shed around the house, and regular vacuuming is the best way to tackle the rest. Owners of heavy shedders are advised to invest in breed-appropriate grooming tools (e.g. a slicker brush, a comb with rotating teeth and a de-matting rake) as well as a specialist vacuum cleaner designed to tackle pet hairs – standard models can choke up completely when faced with, say, a moulting Malamute. To remove clinging hairs from clothes and furniture, roll packing tape around your hand, sticky side outwards, and pat it over the affected area. Or you can use old rubber gloves or a slightly dampened sponge to wipe it off. You can also spray upholstery with static guard products before vacuuming to make your task easier. During periods of heavy moult, it may be advisable to cover furniture with washable throws. Some dogs are quite happy for you to run the hose of the vacuum

cleaner over them as well while you are cleaning, removing loose hairs before they can drop off, but don't try this unless your dog is completely confident about the machine.

Prevention: You can't prevent moulting but, if you really don't want a hairy house, you can choose a breed that keeps its moult to the minimum. A number of breeds are described as 'non-shedding', but the only genuine non-moulters are naked breeds, such as the American Hairless Terrier. For minimal moult consider such breeds as the Poodle, Yorkshire Terrier, Tibetan Terrier, Portuguese Water Dog or most of the rough-coated terrier breeds, but be aware that these dogs still need grooming and in most cases clipping or stripping two or three times a year.

MY DOG DROOLS EVERYWHERE

Causes: All dogs salivate when stressed or overheated, but dogs with loose lips and heavy jowls tend to drool copiously much of the time. Occasional drooling can also be due to dental/oral problems, stress or excitement – or, in the worse case scenario, poisoning.

▲ *You may need to be quick to wipe off strings of drool hanging from your dog's jaws before he can spread them over your clothes, furnishings and guests – keep a dog towel handy.*

Breed notes: The worst offenders include Basset Hounds, Bloodhounds, Bulldogs, Mastiffs, St Bernards *(right)*, Neapolitan Mastiffs and Newfoundlands. An enthusiastic Newfoundland can, with one shake of his head, send a stream of slobber flying six metres across the room!

Action: If your dog is not a habitual drooler, check for sore gums, bad teeth or even a piece of wood or bone lodged in his mouth. If the cause is clearly stress or excitement, work on calming exercises. Drooling may indicate nausea (e.g. in the car, or if your dog has recently eaten something unsuitable). Unexplained one-off drooling, especially if accompanied by other symptoms, should be checked out by the vet.

With regular droolers, you just have to learn to live with it. Keep a supply of dog towels handy to wipe your dog's mouth, especially after meals and when he is excited. Owners of champion dribblers often put bibs on their dogs to catch the dribble and keep their chests dry. Wipe up drool as soon as possible before it leaves stains. A damp cloth will suffice for hard surfaces; fabric will need washing with biological detergent on a cool water cycle (hot water will set the stains); and windows are best tackled with a mixture of white vinegar and water. If you own a breed which drools heavily, you may need to re-plan your furnishings, or restrict your dog to part of the house.

Prevention: You can't stop a drooler drooling, but useful tips include keeping your dog away from the dining table (the smell of food will set him salivating) and keeping his ears clean and mite-free (irritation in the ears will start him shaking his head, sending the drool flying).

MESSY MATTERS

MY DOG LICKS FABRIC

Causes: Licking or sucking bedding, clothes and soft furnishings ('wool-sucking') may be linked with too-early weaning, may be a dietary issue arising from nutritional deficiencies or food allergies, may indicate stress or boredom, and is sometimes an attention-seeking action. Usually it seems to be a comfort habit – like thumb-sucking in humans.

Action: Sometimes simply providing more mental and physical exercise is all that is needed. A dog whose life lacks stimulation seeks comfort habits; a dog whose mind and body have plenty of occupation is more likely to relax and go to sleep. In the meantime, when your dog engages in this undesirable behaviour, follow a policy of interruption and redirection. Don't scold or punish him, which will either increase his stress levels or reward his desire for attention. Interrupt his activity indirectly with a sharp sound, dropping a bunch of keys or any other clattering object. Ideally he should not associate the sound with you, but should be startled (not frightened) into stopping what he is doing. Once he has stopped, call him over for a fuss, a game, a walk or a grooming session – providing an alternative activity. It may also help

▶ *Drop metal discs or some keys with a clatter to interrupt your dog's activity, then offer him a more attractive option.*

to treat fabrics with a pet deterrent spray, which has an unpleasant bitter taste.

Prevention: If your dog starts this habit, try to nip it in the bud before it becomes established.

MY DOG SUCKS OR CHEWS HIS PAWS

This apparently harmless habit can drive owners mad. Confirmed paw-suckers can make just as much of a wet mess of their surroundings as fabric-lickers, and repetitive licking can cause serious damage to the paw.

Causes: Sometimes paw-sucking has a physical cause such as skin irritation, allergy, parasites, joint pain, hypothyroidism (caused by an underactive thyroid gland), or (a common problem) a grass seed embedded between the toes. However, it can also be a comfort habit like fabric-licking (*see above*), and can become obsessive to the point of self-mutilation. There may even be a genetic predisposition.

Breed notes: Breeds with a higher than average tendency to obsessive-compulsive paw-licking include Irish Setters, Labradors, German Shepherds, Great Danes and a number of the toy breeds.

Action: If your dog suddenly starts paw-sucking out of the blue, check immediately for a physical cause so that the problem can be treated. Habitual paw-suckers fall into two groups, those who just make their paws wet and soggy and those who damage themselves. Signs such as hair loss, red and irritated skin, or discoloration of the fur suggest that the licking has become obsessive

and needs to be referred to your vet, who can check for any physical cause and provide treatment if necessary.

If the habit is due to stress, treat like fabric-sucking (*see above*) with increased exercise, interruption and redirection. Try offering your dog a food-stuffed toy whenever he has nothing to do, to provide an appealing alternative to chewing his paws — be sneaky and push a little peanut butter or meat paste deep inside the toy where he can't quite reach it, but can spend hours trying. In severe cases, you may need to consider using bandages or an Elizabethan collar as a short-term measure, or applying deterrent spray on the paws (not advisable if the skin is broken), or your vet may prescribe anti-obsessional medication.

Prevention: Keep your dog busy and happy, and check paw-pads and between the toes on a regular basis, especially in grass-seed season.

MY DOG SCRATCHES CONSTANTLY

Causes: Parasites; allergy; nutritional deficiency; bacterial or fungal infection; habit arising out of stress or boredom. Fleas are one of the commonest culprits: some dogs are allergic to flea bites, and a single bite can cause misery for days.

Action: Consult your vet to establish the cause. You may need to start a regular flea control programme or change your dog's diet — sometimes something as simple as adding a dollop of margarine to his dinner may improve his skin condition. For immediate relief, try bathing your dog with cool water (hot water is likely to irritate the skin further) and use an oatmeal shampoo. If there is no obvious physical cause, try a programme of exercise, or interruption and redirection as explained above.

Prevention: Provide a high-quality diet, keep your dog reasonably clean, and maintain regular flea treatments.

▲ *Country walks can leave grass seeds or mud between your dog's toes, causing discomfort and leading him to chew and lick his feet.*

MESSY MATTERS

MY DOG KEEPS GETTING FLEAS

Cause: Modern flea treatments are very effective but, if you only treat your dog and not his environment, he will quickly become reinfested. Killing the fleas on your dog leaves hundreds of eggs and larvae lurking wherever he goes in your house – each female flea lays some 50 eggs a day, so a household can quickly turn into a flea factory.

Action: You need two types of flea treatment, one to use directly on the dog and one to treat your home. Ask your vet to recommend or supply suitable products, as not all have a long-lasting effect. Before using the household spray, vacuum your home thoroughly to remove as much of the infestation as possible. (Don't forget to destroy the contents of the vacuum cleaner, ideally by burning.) It is also important to read the directions on the spray-can: these will probably include instructions to remove pets such as fish and hamsters from the rooms before spraying, and to leave the room shut up for a period before re-entering. Ensure that you treat every inch of the carpet, including under the furniture, and don't forget to spray under mattresses, along the bottoms of curtains, and on all soft furnishings.

Prevention: Maintain a regular flea treatment programme.

MY DOG HAS A TICK

Cause: These unattractive little blood-sucking parasites are easily picked up by dogs (and their owners) when walking in the countryside.

▲ *Flea-bites itch; without treatment, they can also lead to severe skin problems.*

Action: Ticks should be removed as soon as possible, as they can carry serious diseases. However, never just pull a tick off, as it may break, leaving its mouthparts embedded in the dog's skin where they can cause a nasty sore. Also avoid methods such as burning the tick off with a cigarette (rarely successful, and you may easily burn your dog) or bathing it in surgical spirit, both of which incite the parasite to regurgitate infectious fluids back into its victim. The safest approach is to cover the tick with vaseline, butter or cooking oil (which prevents it from breathing, at best killing it and at worst loosening its grip) and leave it for a couple of hours before tackling it with tweezers, fingernails or a tick remover. Grip

▶ *Ticks come in assorted shapes and sizes – try to learn to recognise them.*

the tick close to the dog's skin, take care not to squeeze it, and pull steadily without twisting. When the tick is out, clean the area with antiseptic. If part of the tick remains in the dog's skin, pick it out with a sterilised needle as you would a splinter, before disinfecting. If you are not confident that you can remove the tick cleanly, ask your vet to do it for you.

Prevention: If your dog is likely to be exposed to ticks, ask your vet for a tick repellant and follow the instructions. Check your dog after country walks, looking for tiny brown or grey lumps or fat pinkish excrescences attached to the skin. (Before feeding ticks are small and dark; after sucking your dog's blood they swell up quite considerably to reach the size of a fat pea.)

MY DOG HAS WORMS

Cause: Dogs pick up a range of internal parasites quite easily – and puppies pick up worms from their mother even before birth. If your dog has not been wormed recently, assume he has worms! Dogs with worms may not show any symptoms until they have a dangerously high infestation; signs that are likely to bring themselves to your attention are wriggling roundworms in faeces and vomit, or white tapeworm segments around the dog's anus.

Action: Puppies should be wormed fortnightly with an age-appropriate wormer from two or three weeks to 12 weeks of age, then monthly until they are six months old. Dogs over six months should be wormed at least three times a year; breeding bitches should be wormed at the time of mating and again a month after they have given birth.

Prevention: Worm your dog regularly, using a preparation recommended by your vet rather than an off-the-shelf purchase. Maintain flea treatment, as fleas can infect your dog with tapeworms. Always pick up your dog's faeces to prevent the spread of infection, keep him away from strays (who won't have been wormed), don't let him eat faeces, and don't let him investigate carrion (a potential source of tapeworms).

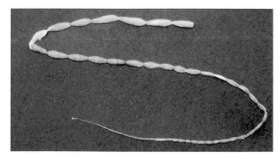

▲ *The canine tapeworm is spread by fleas, and can also infest humans, especially children.*

▶ *It's vital to calculate the right dose of worming tablets for your dog's weight.*

MESSY MATTERS

MY DOG IS VOMITING

Causes: Dogs vomit easily, often without giving cause for concern with causes ranging from minor to serious. Minor causes include eating too fast; eating too much; eating unsuitable foods; grass-eating; motion sickness; worm infestation, especially in puppies. Some dogs have sensitive stomachs and can only cope with a very bland diet. Nursing bitches will regurgitate undigested food for their puppies to eat, and even unrelated dogs may make similar offerings when faced with a young puppy. More serious causes include: heat-stroke; a foreign body lodged in stomach (e.g. tennis ball); stomach tumour (especially in older dogs); kidney and liver disorders; pancreatitis (inflammation of the pancreas); intestinal disorders such as colitis; infections such as parvovirus and distemper; gastric ulcers; poison.

▲ *Grass-eating often causes mild vomiting, which is perfectly normal and no cause for concern.*

Action: All dogs vomit sometimes: there is no need to worry if your dog vomits occasionally and otherwise seems perfectly well. If this is the case, withhold food for 24 hours, and then provide a bland diet, such as chicken or rice, divided into several small meals a day. If he is still vomiting after a couple of days, consult your vet.

Dogs who bolt their food and regularly vomit afterwards often benefit from having the daily ration divided into several small servings over the course of the day. Alternatively, eating too fast can be prevented by placing a rock (too big to be swallowed) in the middle of the bowl so that the dog has to pick round it instead of engulfing huge mouthfuls of food in a hurry. When vomiting is due to roundworm infestation (usually affecting puppies mostly), obviously worming is essential: dogs should be wormed every three months to prevent this problem. If your dog seems to have a sensitive digestion, his diet needs to be adjusted, but take advice from your vet over this: some bland diets (e.g. cooked chicken and rice) may solve the vomiting problem but lead to vitamin and mineral deficiencies. Any dietary changes should be phased in gradually.

Veterinary advice should be sought immediately if vomiting is severe, continuous, contains blood or is accompanied by other symptoms such as diarrhoea, breathing problems, or stomach bloating; if there is reason to suspect poisoning; or if your dog is obviously unwell.

Prevention: Feeding a sensible diet, preventing your dog from scavenging and maintaining regular worm treatments reduces the likelihood of vomiting.

▲ *A stomach bloated by gas is a symptom to take seriously – bloat can be fatal.*

MY DOG ATTEMPTS TO VOMIT BUT BRINGS NOTHING UP

Cause: This is a common symptom of gastric bloat (a painful build-up of gases internally, distending the stomach and often leading to gastric torsion, the twisting round of the stomach which cuts off the blood supply).

Breed notes: Commonest in large, deep-chested breeds, e.g. German Shepherds, Great Danes, Akitas, Mastiffs *(right)* and Bullmastiffs.

Action: Treat as an emergency and call your vet immediately. Gastric torsion is rapidly fatal without veterinary intervention. If you own one of the breeds at risk of gastric torsion, make sure you know your veterinary surgery's emergency number for out-of-hours calls.

Prevention: To reduce the

risk of bloat, don't feed large meals in one sitting, discourage bolting of food and gulping of large amounts of water at mealtimes, and don't exercise your dog within two hours of feeding.

HOW DO I TACKLE VOMIT STAINS?

Action: Canine vomit stains need to be tackled promptly, because the acid content (and the artificial colouring in many pet foods) tends to cause permanent discoloration or carpets and cushions if given time to set. Scrape up solid particles with an old spoon, then soak the area with soda water or plain cold water. Leave for 30 seconds, then blot dry with paper towels as thoroughly as possible. Repeat the process two or three times. If the area remains discoloured, use a biological stain remover designed for pet stains. For an alternative approach, after scraping up all solids, sprinkle the area with baking soda and leave it to dry thoroughly before vacuuming and then treating with soda water or cold water as above. Old stains which have set into the carpet can usually be reduced, if not removed entirely, by steam-cleaning.

Neapolitan Mastiff

SEXUAL STIRRINGS

'Sexual misconduct' by your dog may have very little to do with sex to the canine mind, but is often more to do with establishing social status or even a perfectly polite greeting in doggy language. In sexual matters, dogs have the same innocent tactlessness as the small child who wants to discuss the facts of life at full volume on a crowded bus, and, like children, they need to learn appropriate manners.

MY DOG MOUNTS OTHER DOGS

Causes: Mounting is usually more about status than about sex (except in the case of adolescents, when it may well be part of a range of less than desirable behaviour patterns stirred up by raging hormones). If this behaviour features regularly and to the irritation of other dogs, your dog has almost certainly missed out on canine social life and has never learned the place and time for

▶ *Mounting behaviour is part of the normal puppy play curriculum, as youngsters establish social rules.*

dominant behaviour. Just like children, dogs need to meet and mingle with others of their kind to learn how to socialise properly. In puppies (say under six months), mounting is part of normal social play behaviour, during which pups learn about status and appropriate conduct. In adults, it is usually an attempt to establish dominant status and, if overdone, suggests that your dog is insecure in his role among other dogs.

Action: Your dog needs to spend time with other, well-socialised dogs, who can discourage this type of behaviour and teach him proper canine manners. Check out local training classes, looking for one with a dog-friendly, reward-based approach, where other dog owners can help you with this problem. Spending time on training is essential, so that you can at least call your dog back to you if he is annoying other canines. Castration is unlikely to affect a learned behaviour pattern, so don't expect your vet to solve matters for you.

Prevention: Help your puppy to grow up into a well-socialised dog by taking him to puppy classes and allowing him to mix with other dogs in the park as soon as his vaccinations take effect.

MY DOG HUMPS PEOPLE'S LEGS

Causes: Much the same applies as above – dogs tend to regard human family and friends as part of the pack, and will apply dominant behaviour such as mounting if they are unsure of their place in the pack hierarchy.

Action: Interrupt this behaviour as soon as it occurs by clapping your hands loudly or snapping out a sharp 'No', following this up by leading your dog away from the situation. Never haul or kick him off his victim, as you may cause injury and certainly will cause confusion in his mind by punishing him for what he sees as acceptable canine conduct. If he is prone to poking his nose where it doesn't belong, keep him on the lead when you have visitors so that he doesn't have a chance to exhibit undesirable behaviour. **Prevention:** Work on your dog's training, so that he feels comfortable with his place in the family. Don't let visitors over-excite your pet – always a temptation where playful puppies and young dogs are concerned – but teach him that other people are to be treated with courtesy. A dog who is trained to sit to greet visitors is a much more desirable pet than one who views other people as there for his amusement.

need to teach your dog what counts as good manners in canine-human encounters.

Action: With a dog prone to this behaviour, keep him on the lead when in company, and each time he makes for the forbidden zone ask him to sit instead, then reward him. Pushing him away won't teach him anything, as many dogs will find this attention rewarding in itself, while shouting at him will merely confuse him.

Prevention: Teach your dog appropriate alternative behaviour when meeting and greeting people, such as sitting and offering a paw.

MY DOG MAKES STRAIGHT FOR PEOPLE'S CROTCHES

Causes: This is natural dog behaviour, and counts as good manners in canine circles! You now

◀ An inappropriate greeting – this dog is not going to be a favourite with your friends!

▲ A much more acceptable way for a dog to greet humans, and one that friends will appreciate.

SEXUAL STIRRINGS

MY DOG HUMPS TOYS AND CUSHIONS

Causes: Sex play is normal in adolescent dogs, at the age when they experience a surge in hormones, and to a lesser extent in adults. If the habit persists into adult life, this may be due to boredom (the dog has nothing more interesting to do), attention-seeking (on the principle that it is better to be told off than ignored) or itching or irritation in the genital area – or of course you may have an individual with a high sex drive.

▲ If your dogs regards soft toys as an invitation to sex play, try to focus his attention on a less stimulating item, such as a rubber ball.

Action: Most of us want our cushions to be treated with respect and prefer our dogs not to hump their toys in front of visitors, so it is best to tackle this problem early on. Scolding or punishing the dog is usually counter-productive: it is better to redirect his attention elsewhere. The more time you spend training and playing with your dog, the more eager he will be to leave what he is doing and take up another activity, enabling you to call him away from his sex play to sit quietly beside you or play a more respectable game

with his favourite toy. With persistent offenders, you may need to interrupt the undesirable activity: keep a spray bottle full of water handy and, whenever you see your dog assaulting a cushion or toy, tell him 'No' and squirt a jet of water at him. Follow this up with an interesting distraction so that stopping his sex play is rewarding for him. You can also protect cushions by treating them every few days with a scent deterrent spray. Don't expect neutering to work as a cure for this habit once established; re-direction will still be necessary.

Prevention: Expect adolescent dogs (especially but not exclusively males) to go through a phase of inappropriate mounting, and be ready to deflect and distract.

MY DOG IS A FLASHER

Cause: It's quite natural for a male dog to get an erection when excited, sexually or otherwise. Normally this isn't a problem; but some young, excitable dogs do tend to flash their equipment in any social gathering, which can become an embarrassment to their owners – especially with large, short-coated breeds.

Action: As with cushion-humping, you may be able to discourage flashing by distracting your dog, either with a quick spray of water or with the temptation of an appealing activity. However, there is no real 'quick fix' solution for this problem: you need to work towards having a dog who is calm and relaxed in social situations, which means spending time on more exercise and more training. Many pet dogs are under-exercised and under-stimulated, which increases any tendency to become over-excited on outings or when meeting visitors.

Prevention: Complete prevention of a natural physical reaction is impossible, but keeping your dog's mind and body busy will usually keep arousal down to an acceptable level.

MY DOG LICKS HIS GENITALS NOISILY IN PUBLIC

Causes: Licking the genitals is part of basic canine hygiene, but some dogs do it to excess. This may be set off by discomfort in the genital area arising from an injury or skin irritation, genital discharge, urinary incontinence, etc., which can often be exacerbated by excessive licking. The habit can also arise out of stress or boredom, or indeed can become an attention-seeking display if the owner responds to it with attention, so don't over-react

Action: If you find any injury, skin irritation, lumps and bumps or genital discharge, seek veterinary attention promptly. Otherwise, aim to distract your dog as soon as he starts licking, providing some more rewarding activity such as a game, a walk or a fun training

▲ With short-haired dogs, it's easy to spot any physical problems early on – long-haired dogs need conscientious check-ups.

session. Never ignore obsessive self-licking, as it can lead to sores and wounds which are hard to treat.

Prevention: Frequent regular health checks (easily carried out while grooming your dog) will help you to spot physical disorders, such as genital discharge, early on; and keeping your dog's mind and body busy will reduce the likelihood of neurotic behaviour, such as obsessive licking.

◄ Excessive licking of any area needs tackling promptly to prevent worse problems.

SEXUAL STIRRINGS

MY MALE DOG GOES WANDERING IN SEARCH OF BITCHES

Cause: It's your dog's nature to follow the scent of any bitch who is on heat – or, if he is a real Romeo, who might possibly be on heat sometime in the future. It is your responsibility to escape-proof your home to protect him from the risks of wandering off. If you let him roam, he will be in danger of being lost, stolen, impounded, injured or even killed; he will also be a traffic hazard and a public nuisance, and you should not forget the legal implications should he cause an accident while out.

Action: Keep him in! Escape-proof your house and garden, and walk him on a leash. However, this merely contains the problem rather than solving it. You need also to find him something else to think about apart from sex, which means increasing his physical and mental exercise. If sex is always on his mind, you should consider castration, which solves the problem in the majority of cases and will make him not only an easier companion

◀ *The dog's sensitive nose can detect a possible mate from miles away.*

to live with but also a happier dog, freed from constant frustration.

Prevention: Early castration is the only certain preventative. However, most entire (un-castrated) dogs who are not regularly exposed to bitches on heat and not used for breeding will not spend time actively seeking a mate, and if you never let your dog wander off to find his own amusements he cannot develop this habit.

MY MALE DOG WEES INDOORS WHEN EXCITED BY MEETING BITCHES

Cause: Territorial marking is a normal reaction to meeting a potential mate.

Action: If you know your dog is reacting strongly to female acquaintances, supervise him closely after the meeting and 'hit' him with a sharp 'No!' at the first sign of him lifting his leg, rushing him outside immediately and encouraging him to cock his leg in approved surroundings. You may have to repeat this practice several times before training takes

◀ *A dog can't wander off if he is kept secure at home and walked only on-leash.*

Prevention: Again, early castration is the only way of ensuring that your dog never adopts this habit, and later castration will reduce or stop this behaviour in many males. However, many male dogs go through their entire lives without putting a paw wrong in this way.

MY FEMALE DOG DISPLAYS MALE SEXUAL BEHAVIOUR

Cause: It's normal for puppies of both sexes to display mounting behaviour (humping cushions and toys, *right*) when excited. This is part of the inborn vocabulary of canine body language (remember that, among dogs, mounting behaviour is often a statement of social status rather than a sexual activity). Most female puppies will outgrow the practice, though it may recur when they are coming into season as hormonal changes affect behaviour. However, high-ranking bitches – the naturally dominant type, and also those who acquire status, say as the only and therefore 'top' bitch in a multi-dog household – often continue to display mounting behaviour. If this becomes a problem, treat as with male dogs (*see My dog humps toys and cushions, p.54*). Less commonly, high-status bitches may also imitate males by cocking a leg when urinating in order to position scent-marks higher. Fortunately, they are less obsessive than males about leaving their mark and much less prone to lift a leg on the furniture.

over from instinct. The use of a water pistol is sometimes recommended as a quick deterrent, giving your dog a short cold shock whenever he starts to lift his leg, but unless you can squirt him from somewhere out of sight, he is more likely to associate the unpleasant experience with you than

◀ *The deterrent water-pistol treatment can be messy itself.*

with his own actions – and some of the water is bound to hit your carpet or furniture. It is essential to clean up after every incident, removing all scent traces of his mistakes with an ammonia-free cleaner, so that he is not cued by his sense of smell to return to the same site and repeat his performance.

SEXUAL STIRRINGS

MY FEMALE DOG GETS MOODY WHEN IN SEASON

Cause: Many unspayed bitches undergo changes of mood and behaviour just prior to, during, and just after their heat period. They may become irritable, nervous, aggressive, or over-affectionate and clingy. They may lose interest in food or start urinating in the house, and are often restless and eager to escape to find a mate. This is all due to the hormonal changes associated with coming into season.

Action: Unless you intend to breed from your bitch, spaying is the obvious answer. It is possible to prevent your bitch from coming into season with hormone treatment – usually an injection every five months (see p.62) – but this does have some health implications and should not be considered a permanent solution.

Prevention: Spaying will prevent this problem and make life pleasanter for both you and your dog.

HOW DO I PREVENT UNWANTED PREGNANCY WHEN MY BITCH IS IN SEASON?

Action: Bitches usually come into season for the first time sometime after the age of six months, and thereafter typically twice a year (once a year in some breeds). Each heat period lasts some three to four weeks. A bitch is most likely to be successfully mated in the period between day 7 and day 15, but individuals vary, so to avoid accidental pregnancy she must be segregated for the whole period. While she is in season, she should be securely confined at any times that you cannot provide close supervision. Her exercise will have to be limited, as she will attract males from a considerable distance whenever she goes out.

If you do walk her, if at all possible carry her to the car and drive away from home for the walk, keeping her on the lead at all times, carrying her back from the car again when you return home – this will prevent her from leaving a scent trail to your door and attracting every stray in the neighbourhood.

▼ A bitch in season leaves a scent trail for males – unless you carry her.

just as if they were truly pregnant. Symptoms may include mothering inanimate objects (toys, slippers, etc), nest-making, lethargy and poor appetite, aggression, weight increase, swollen teats, milk production, and even appearing to go into labour. Of course, these same symptoms may also mean that your bitch has been mated without your knowledge and is really pregnant.

Action: If there is any chance that your bitch might have been accidentally mated, ask your vet to check her condition. If she is indeed pregnant, she will need an appropriate diet and worming treatment. If it is merely a false pregnancy, there is usually no need for treatment. Try to distract her from acting out her maternal instincts and encourage her to go for walks, play and generally interact with the household as usual. A minority

▲ *If your bitch is in season, canine suitors will turn up out of the blue whenever you take her out.*

Be paranoid: male dogs can smell her miles off and appear from nowhere. Never leave her unattended in the garden, as she will be strongly motivated to find escape routes which were not apparent before, and passing males will be equally keen on finding a way in. Constant vigilance is the rule! In a multi-dog household she must be totally isolated from uncastrated male companions, even if you think these are too young or too old to present a threat. Be aware that any male dogs in the house are likely to be frustrated and unhappy at this time and present with behavioural problems of their own.

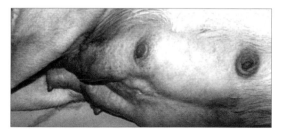

▲ *Swollen teats, perhaps producing milk, may mean a false pregnancy – or a genuine one.*

of cases will need veterinary assistance. If your bitch seems unwell, is off her food for more than 24 hours, develops a vaginal discharge or starts coming heavily into milk, see the vet. False pregnancies tend to recur with subsequent heats, so unless there are good reasons to attempt to breed from your bitch in the future, you should consider having her spayed once the false pregnancy is over and hormone production is back to normal.

Prevention: Spaying will prevent this problem occurring.

MY FEMALE DOG IS ACTING ODDLY AFTER HER SEASON

Causes: False pregnancy; genuine pregnancy. Some bitches experience a false or 'phantom' pregnancy, undergoing physical and/or psychological changes

SEXUAL STIRRINGS

SHOULD I HAVE MY BITCH SPAYED?

Unless you have good reason for breeding from your bitch, the answer is probably a resounding Yes. It will improve the quality of her life, save you a lot of worry, and is a responsible approach to the problem of canine over-population.

Thousands of hopeful puppies end up in dog pounds and rescues – or worse.

Advantages: Your dog will not contribute to the surplus of puppies born each year – there are always many more puppies than good homes available. She will no longer come into season, so you will not have to cope with any mess or inconvenience, the need to keep her under close guard for three-week periods twice a year, the mood-swings some bitches have when in heat, canine Romeos hanging around your door, or false pregnancies. Spaying removes a number of health hazards, such as pyometra (a life-threatening uterine infection) and ovarian cancer, and, if carried out before your bitch is two years old, reduces the risk of mammary cancer.

Disadvantages: Spaying may be linked to urinary incontinence later in life, although this can be controlled by medication. In certain long-haired breeds, such as spaniels and setters, spaying often changes the growth of the coat, producing a softer, fluffy or woolly coat which needs more grooming and may not appeal to owners. Spaying of dominant bitches can make them even more dominant and worsen any aggressive behaviour. Although spaying won't actually make your dog fat (guide dogs are routinely neutered, and they have to remain fit), it will slow down her metabolism so that she needs less food, and you will need to monitor her diet.

▲ This spaniel bitch's coat is softer and fluffier than normal as a side-effect of spaying.

SHOULD I HAVE MY MALE DOG CASTRATED?

Unless you have good reason for breeding from your dog, most vets and charities would say Yes, because they regularly have to deal with the consequences of accidental matings. However, many owners can point to well-supervised male dogs who have never sired a litter and who show no signs of frustration or sex-related misbehaviour. Castration is recommended in certain cases, e.g. dogs with behavioural problems linked with male hormones, such as dominant aggression, dogs who regularly mix with unspayed bitches, and dogs with one or both testicles undescended, who run a high risk of testicular cancer. Beyond that, it is a matter of choice.

Advantages: Your dog will not contribute to the surplus of puppies born each year – there are always many more puppies than good homes available. Castration doesn't change a dog's personality, although if carried out before the dog is fully adult (at, say, two or three years old) it usually makes them calmer and easier to train. It reduces interest in the opposite sex and sex-related misbehaviour, such as cocking a leg on the

furniture, humping cushions and ankles and legs, and roaming, although if these habits are well-established castration needs to be supported by re-training. In most cases, it lessens aggression (unless this is fear-based), territoriality and over-excitability. Castrated dogs urinate less frequently, so walks won't be dominated by constant pauses to mark gate-posts. The castrated dog won't be frustrated by the scent of bitches in season which he is not permitted to approach. Castration removes the risk of testicular cancer, anal adenoma (a type of tumour) and perineal hernia (a hernia near the anus) and reduces the risk of prostate problems in later life.

Disadvantages: Although castration generally makes dogs easier to handle, it should not be viewed as a cure-all for behavioural problems.

Castration of dogs displaying fear-based aggression is likely to aggravate the problem. In certain long-haired breeds, such as spaniels and setters, castration often changes the growth of the coat, producing a softer, fluffy or woolly coat which needs more grooming and may not appeal to owners. Some castrated dogs become sexually

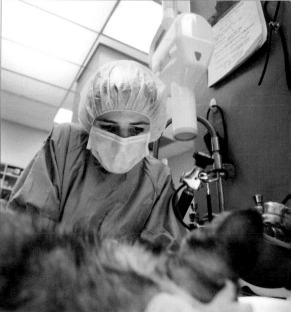

▲ *Neutering is carried out by a qualified vet and carries only minimal physical risks.*

attractive to other males after the operation, which can be distressing to the dog concerned as well as inconvenient to the owner. One study suggests that castrated males are more likely to suffer cognitive impairment in old age than entire males. Although castration won't actually make your dog fat (guide dogs are routinely neutered, and they have to remain fit), it will slow down his metabolism so that he needs less food, and you will need to monitor his diet.

SEXUAL STIRRINGS

WHAT ABOUT CHEMICAL NEUTERING?

As alternatives to surgery, hormone injections can be used for temporary 'chemical castration' of dogs and to prevent bitches coming into season.

Chemical castration: This is an anti-testosterone injection which has the same effect as surgical castration, but is temporary (lasting about a month). If you are considering neutering as a means of altering your dog's behaviour (e.g. dominant or inter-male aggression, roaming, and sexual misdemeanours), a month's chemical castration enables you to assess whether it is likely to be effective. It is also a means of treating prostate problems if you are reluctant to have your dog permanently castrated. However, it is not effective as a means of contraception, as your dog may still be able to mate and sire a litter, and should certainly not be considered as a long-term option.

Heat-suppressing hormones: Treatment to stop a bitch coming on heat may be administered by injections or in tablet form. This completely suppresses her season and all its attendant problems: she will not attract males, become pregnant or undergo mood swings. Its effect is temporary, so she remains available for breeding in the future; regular treatments (typically every five months) will be needed to prevent her coming into season when she is next due. There are disadvantages. Some bitches may suffer side effects, some develop a false pregnancy after treatment and require a further injection, a few fail to come back into season when treatment is discontinued, and, unlike spaying, it leaves a bitch vulnerable to such disorders as pyometra. It is not recommended for use before a bitch has had her first season. On the whole it is most useful as a one-off emergency measure, for example if you have booked a holiday and need to put your bitch into kennels when her season is due.

WHAT IS THE BEST AGE FOR NEUTERING?

Most vets have decided views on the subject, but these views differ! Some favour early neutering before secondary sexual characteristics develop, while others prefer to allow a dog or bitch to mature physically before spaying or castration.

Early neutering: Neutering before puberty (anywhere from six months

Hormone injections have a short-term effect.

▼ *Your vet will be happy to discuss this option with you.*

in toy breeds to 24 months in large breeds) is favoured by many vets and rescue schemes, and some opt for neutering as early as six weeks. Dogs who are neutered early are less likely to be aggressive and tend to remain puppyish and playful even when mature. Some early-neutered males may never learn to cock a leg, but continue to squat to urinate.

Early neutering may have a 'Peter Pan' effect on a dog's character.

   Spaying a bitch before her first season considerably reduces the risk of mammary cancer in later life, but may increase the risk of urinary incontinence. In both sexes, neutering before puberty affects adult appearance by causing bone growth to continue past the normal age, resulting in a taller, lighter-boned and longer-legged animal. Bitches may have a rather masculine appearance when mature, while males may appear rather feminine. The change of bone proportion also leads to an increased risk of ruptured ligaments and hip dysplasia (dislocation of the hip joint). Studies suggest that early neutering is associated with decreased separation anxiety, obesity, escapology, and inappropriate urination, but increased fearful behaviour, male aggression, noise phobias and sexual misbehaviour.

Post-pubertal neutering: Many owners prefer to wait until their pet has completed his or her physical development – in the case of a bitch, until she has had her first season and her organs have had time to mature. This does mean that you have to be on the alert for her first heat from about five months onwards, and take care to segregate her for the full period that she is fertile.

It also slightly increases the risk of mammary cancer in later life, but not as much as if she is not spayed at all. With dogs, the usual reason for castration is to tackle behavioural problems, and the older he is at the time of neutering, the less effect the operation will have on his behaviour. Bad habits are learned as well as hormone-driven, so castration works better as an early preventative than as a cure. However, there is no upper age limit for neutering.

▲ *Neutering can be carried out at any age: it is up to you to make an informed decision on timing.*

SEXUAL STIRRINGS

WILL IT AFFECT MY DOG'S TEMPERAMENT IF I ALLOW HIM TO BE USED AT STUD?

Probably. Dogs don't miss what they have never had, but once your dog has had experience of mating, his interest in the opposite sex will almost certainly increase. He may also regard himself as being of higher status than before and become less responsive to his owner.

◀ Don't expect your companion dog to be a stud dog as well.

▲ *Only an X-ray can prove whether a dog who seems sound is at risk from hip dysplasia.*

It's tempting when you have a good dog and a friend suggests breeding him to their bitch, but you run the risk of damaging your relationship with your dog, with no guarantee that the mating will result in the desired puppies. In any case, it is inadvisable to breed from any dog or bitch unless you know the bloodlines, have carried out appropriate health checks before considering mating, and can ensure good homes for the puppies and back-up for their new owners.

wives' tale. There is no medical or psychological benefit to the bitch, and there are already far more puppies in existence than there are good homes available. If you are thinking in terms of keeping one puppy to perpetuate your bitch's bloodlines, be aware that there is no guarantee that the puppy will take after its mother! To avoid adding to the canine over-population problem, don't breed a litter unless:

- You are knowledgeable about dogs.
- Your bitch and the chosen sire are physically sound and of good temperament.
- Both your bitch and the chosen sire have tested clear of all inherited problems (e.g. eye problems and hip dysplasia).
- You have the funds to cover rearing the litter (including worming and vaccinations) and also any veterinary emergencies (e.g. caesarean delivery).
- You have time to care for the puppies, including weaning, house-training and socialisation. Puppies need to be accustomed to a range of experiences from being introduced to noisy vacuum cleaners to

SHOULD I LET MY BITCH HAVE ONE LITTER?

The popular theory that a bitch should be allowed to have one litter before being spayed is an old

being picked up and handled before they leave their mother if they are to cope well with the outside world.

- You have good homes waiting for them, and are prepared to vet potential owners for suitability.
- You have the capacity to take back any pups whose owners for one reason or another cannot keep them. If one of your pups is unlucky, this could mean taking back into your home a mature dog who has developed all sorts of behavioural, or indeed medical, problems – but a responsible breeder has to be prepared for such an eventuality.

▲ Raising puppies is a time-consuming task. They need hours of attention and supervision.

MY BITCH HAS BEEN ACCIDENTALLY MATED

Cause: Inadequate supervision of bitch in season. Some bitches make life harder for their owners by having what is known as a 'silent' heat, i.e. coming into season so inconspicuously that mere humans fail to notice – although any male dogs in the area certainly will.

Action: Ring your vet immediately. Assuming that you are aware of the mating, you have three options: have your bitch spayed, ask your vet to terminate her pregnancy, or allow her to have the puppies. (If you were not aware of the mating until her pregnancy became obvious, the third option may be the only one available.) The decision to let her have puppies should not be taken lightly. Remember that you will need to provide special care for her during and after pregnancy, there are health risks during pregnancy and birth, puppies are time-consuming and surprisingly expensive to rear, and you will be responsible for finding good homes for them. If you do not plan to breed from your bitch in the future, spaying in early pregnancy (by the third or fourth week) is probably the best solution, ensuring that the problem will not recur. Injections to terminate a pregnancy need to be given as soon as possible, ideally in the first week, and will not affect the bitch's breeding capacity. However, be aware that very occasionally they may not have the desired result and the pregnancy may continue to term, although it is unlikely to result in live puppies.

Prevention: Spaying is recommended; unspayed bitches need close supervision when in season and even when they are due to come into season, to be on the safe side.

▲ Raising puppies is hard work for a bitch, so she will need extra care and attention.

PROBLEMS WITH PEOPLE

Dogs aren't born with good social manners – they have to learn them. Bad experiences with people or lack of early socialisation will produce a dog who doesn't know how to behave among humans, but so will inadequate or confusing training. Dogs need clear, consistent education – just like children.

Telephone trouble!

Dogs need to learn that they can't always have attention on demand.

demands attention – avoid eye contact, turn away, and ignore him. A little later when he is quiet, call him to you and give him some fuss or play. When you're ready, tell him 'Enough,' shut off eye contact and turn away. Be consistent, and he will learn manners. It will help if he also learns to enjoy 'time out'. Teach him to go to his bed, a blanket (which you can move around as suits you), or a crate – using reward-based training to ensure he views this as a refuge, not as a place of banishment. If you have a highly active dog, you should provide him with some occupation such as a food-stuffed toy. It's also important to ensure that he has enough exercise and stimulation during the day, so that his 'time out' is a welcome rest period rather than a stint of boredom.

With puppies, it's rarely a good idea to ignore

▼ *Teaching your dog to go to bed on command is useful in many situations.*

Treats help with training.

MY DOG KEEPS DEMANDING ATTENTION

Cause: Dogs like attention, and they need attention – but they also need to learn that they can't demand it all the time. If you don't teach your dog this lesson, not only will he make a nuisance of himself but he will also become quite stressed because he has not learned to relax in company.

Action: Don't respond when your dog

them for very long – left to their own devices, they will seek entertainment, usually along destructive lines. If you are busy, ensure that your puppy is safely contained (in a crate, puppy pen, or allocated 'secure' room where there is nothing that he can damage or be damaged by) for the necessary period.

Prevention: First, ensure that your dog really does have enough attention. If he is alone and/or bored most of the time, he is going to be a nuisance when the opportunity arises. Second, establish as part of his routine quiet periods when he can relax or enjoy peaceful activities (such as gnawing a bone or tackling a food-stuffed toy) and understands that he should not bother you for the moment.

MY DOG JUMPS UP AT ME

Cause: This is a puppyish canine greeting combining welcome and food-begging. If your dog finds this behaviour rewarding, he will carry it on into adult life, when it is often annoying and sometimes frightening or even dangerous – a big dog can easily knock someone over.

Make jumping up unrewarding for your dog.

Action: When your dog jumps up, don't acknowledge him. Avoid eye contact, fold your arms and turn away (turning sideways offers a smaller target). Don't scold him or push him away, which is counter-productive, as most dogs prefer any response to none. (Equally, avoid old-fashioned practices such as stepping on the dog's feet or kneeing him in the chest – it's hardly appropriate to hurt him for being pleased to see you.) When he gives up and has all four feet on the ground, then praise him. If he responds by jumping up again, repeat the freeze treatment. The goal is to teach him that he will only be greeted when he has all four feet on the ground. Consistency is essential – don't let family or friends undo your good work. If you are quite happy for your dog to jump up at you (as may well be the case with small breeds), teach him to do so only upon invitation, so that you can enjoy his greeting when you want to, but avoid it when he is wet and muddy and you are wearing your best outfit.

Prevention: Don't let the habit start. Crouch to receive a puppy's greeting, so that you don't stimulate him to reach upwards; only reciprocate when he has all four feet on the floor.

PROBLEMS WITH PEOPLE

MY DOG JUMPS UP AT OTHER PEOPLE IN THE PARK

Cause: You have a happy, friendly dog who likes people – and who has no manners! This is a habit that must be tackled as a matter of urgency, as passers-by may be frightened or hurt, especially if your dog is big and heavy.

Action: Walk your dog on a lead and work on keeping him focused on you. Carry food treats or a favourite toy, talk to him in an excited tone of voice, and encourage eye contact. When someone passes, check your dog lightly with the lead to prevent him approaching them and reward the return of his attention to you. Once he is well-behaved on-leash, you can move on to an extending lead and continue the exercise.

▶ *A well-behaved dog greets a friend with all four feet on the ground – and earns a reward.*

Before progressing to off-leash time, persuade a couple of friends to act as stooges, walking past and repelling any advances by turning away (see *My dog jumps up at me, p.67*), while you reinforce the message with a light check of the lead. With a confirmed jumper-up at other people, a remote-controlled spray collar that releases a pungent-smelling spray may help, but you will need to keep a constant watch on your dog and have quick reactions to time the use of the spray correctly.

Prevention: Teach your dog to greet people with all four feet on the ground. Watch out for over-friendly dog-lovers in the park who may welcome your adorable puppy's boisterous advances and inadvertently teach him to jump up at everyone he meets.

▶ *Pawing his owner's leg didn't work, so he sits and looks at her. Now he can be rewarded – and he will soon learn the rules.*

MY DOG KEEPS PAWING AT ME

Cause: Your dog wants attention and has found that this method works.

Action: Make sure this action *doesn't* work. Ignore him; don't make eye contact; back off. If sitting, get up and walk away without acknowledging the dog. You may have to do this repeatedly until the message sinks in.

Prevention: Don't let the habit start. When your puppy paws at you for the first time, it's cute;

▶ *Nobody likes a noisy dog – especially neighbours!*

when your adult dog keeps scrabbling at you when you're busy, it's annoying – and when a full-grown Labrador thumps you with his heavy paw, it hurts! Ignore the cute little paws to establish that this behaviour is unrewarded. When your puppy has given up and is being good and quiet, that is the time to reward his behaviour by calling him for a fuss.

MY DOG KEEPS BARKING AND WHINING AT ME

Cause: Your dog wants attention and has found that this method works.

Action: Once again, you should be able to tackle this problem (with lots of patience) by ignoring the undesirable behaviour and then giving your dog the desired attention once he is quiet. However, some dogs can keep up their vocal demands for a very long time, and it can be quite hard to ignore persistent barking and whining – especially if it's loud enough to annoy the neighbours. In such cases, you may need to take a more active approach. Different approaches work with different dogs. Try saying a firm 'No', then walk away; most dogs get the message after several repetitions. With determined barkers, it can be effective to back up your command with a quick spray of water in the face. Some dogs respond well to a noisy interruption. Provide yourself with a small tin filled with pebbles, a heavy bunch of keys, training discs or any other clattering object, which you can toss on the ground (ideally in such a way that your dog does not see you throw it) when he starts the undesired behaviour. This method is not recommended for sound-sensitive or nervous dogs.

Prevention: Never reward barking or whining with attention of any kind – even if this means delaying a meal or a walk. However, do make sure that you do pay your dog enough attention when he is behaving himself, so that he learns that desirable behaviour is rewarded. Schedule slots of time for play, exercise, training and cuddles every day when your dog has your undivided attention.

▼ *It's just as important to ensure your dog has the attention he needs, and deserves, at appropriate times, as it is to teach him not to demand attention all the time.*

Time for a bit of a fuss.

Playtime is a time for learning too.

PROBLEMS WITH PEOPLE

TROUBLE WHEN PEOPLE CALL

Dogs are social creatures, and most pet dogs thoroughly enjoy seeing visitors when they come to your house. Unfortunately, visitors may not enjoy meeting your dog if he hasn't learned good manners. Over-exuberant welcomes involving jumping, licking and pawing can be just as off-putting to callers as frenzied barking or outright aggression, and need to be tackled just as much as these latter problem behaviours.

most terriers) are geared to bark and bounce at the least excuse, and need more training to be quiet than placid breeds.

Action: Tackling a confirmed barker is often much harder than many behaviourists claim, and it is usually easier to teach your dog a new, alternative behaviour than to try and eliminate his existing habit. Forget the doorbell problem for the moment, and concentrate on teaching your dog to go to his bed on command. It's important to use a

MY DOG GOES MAD WHEN VISITORS RING THE DOORBELL

Causes: Territorial instincts; guard instincts; nervousness of strangers; a naturally vocal breed; boredom leading dog to over-react to any stimulus; lack of training.
Breed notes: Some breeds (e.g. many Spitz breeds, *left*) are more vocal than others. Highly reactive breeds (e.g.

▲ *Teach your dog that dogs don't answer doors: people do. Use a collar and lead if necessary to stop him barging ahead to the door, and work on teaching him to go to his bed instead.*

reward-based approach rather than force, because ultimately you want your dog to regard sitting quietly in his bed as more rewarding than barking at the door. Be patient and teach the desired behaviour in stages: start by going over to his bed and holding a treat over it, handing it to him when he gets into the bed, then move on to standing a little way from the bed and giving the command,

MY DOG PESTERS VISITORS FOR ATTENTION

Cause: Dogs like attention. Often the problem was caused in the first place by visitors making a huge fuss of your cute new puppy – who will then expect the same treatment from every caller.

Action: Keep your dog on the lead when visitors come, ask them to ignore him, and get him to lie down beside you while you chat. Have a pot of training treats to hand so that you can reward him for good behaviour. When this practice is established as routine, ask a sensible friend to call round and help with the next stage. After you and your friend have chatted for a while, drop the leash and ask your friend to call the dog over and pet him calmly for a little, and then to tell him, 'That's enough now,' stop petting him and end eye contact. At this point call your dog back to you, using the trailing lead to draw him back if necessary. With repetition, he will learn to enjoy attention from your visitors without demanding it.

Prevention: Follow the above routine from the start.

waiting until he gets in and then going over to him with his reward. When he has learned to go to bed on command, you can start teaching him to stay there for gradually increasing periods. It will take time and a great deal of repetition to establish this behaviour as a reliable habit, but this is an exercise which will be of benefit in many circumstances and is well worth the effort.

Once he has the idea, arrange for friends to call round and ring the doorbell during training sessions, telling him to go to his bed as soon as the bell rings and rewarding even partial obedience with a particularly tasty treat. Eventually he will learn to go to his bed when he hears the bell, rather than waiting for you to tell him to do so. Of course, although nobody likes a dog who barks incessantly, many dog owners appreciate having a dog who sounds the alert when the doorbell rings. If this is what you want, reward your dog for barking once or twice at the door, then follow up with the command 'Bed,' and give a further reward for this. Most dogs will soon learn what is required.

Prevention: Train puppies from the start not to over-react to the sound of visitors at the door. You may need to stick a note on the door warning callers that you may be slow to respond because you are teaching your dog door manners!

▶ *Not all visitors want an enthusiastic canine greeting, so teach your dog to await an invitation.*

PROBLEMS WITH PEOPLE

AGGRESSION AND TIMIDITY

If you like visitors, but your dog doesn't, it can severely curtail your social life! Having a dog who frightens your friends is antisocial, and indeed if your dog shows aggressive behaviour this can escalate into a real danger. Dogs who are frightened of your friends can be just as distressing, so it is important to teach your dog to be calm with callers.

innate distrust of strangers, and need good early socialisation and sensible handling to make them suitable to live amongst humans.

Action: Get expert help in re-training/socialising your dog. **Never ignore this problem:** it is irresponsible to keep a dangerous dog and do nothing about it. In the meantime, protect visitors (and make a fearful-aggressive dog feel safer) by setting up nursery gates across doors, so that the dog can see people but not reach them. With all but the most aggressive dogs, this is a better temporary solution than shutting your pet away in another room every time visitors call, which often leads to the problem escalating.

Prevention: Proper puppy socialisation is essential to enable dogs to learn how to cope with strange people and situations. This includes training visitors how to behave towards your new puppy as well as vice versa: it may be advisable to accustom your puppy to using a crate as a refuge if you are likely to have uncooperative guests.

▲ Aggressive dogs are rarely happy dogs, and visitors certainly won't be happy to meet them.

MY DOG IS AGGRESSIVE TO VISITORS

Causes: Lack of socialisation; fear of strangers; innate strong guard instincts which the dog has not been taught how to direct; learned bullying behaviour ('Oh wow, this person is scared of me – what fun!').

Breed notes: Guard breeds (e.g. Rottweiler, Akita) have a strong guard drive, often coupled with an

MY DOG IS SCARED OF VISITORS

Causes: Lack of socialisation; negative experience (not necessarily

▶ Cuddles may confirm fears, not allay them.

active mistreatment – a dog who is frightened by, say, a car back-firing outside when a visitor is present may associate the fear with guests in the house); inherited timidity.

Action: Coaxing and comforting a frightened dog is often counter-productive. In effect, you are rewarding his behaviour, and also confirming his impression that the situation really is scary. Generally it pays better to act confidently and be more casual about his fear – if you aren't scared, why should he be? Make sure he has a safe den to hide in if he wants to, and otherwise ignore him when you have visitors.

Gentleness is important with shy dogs.

◀ *A dog who is fearful of people suffers distress, and may progress to becoming a fear-biter.*

▲ *Pick your new dog's first visitors with care, so that encounters are a positive experience for him.*

If he is only shy and timid, he should gradually develop the confidence to investigate the situation. At such times you should ask your visitors to move slowly and gently, keep their voices quiet and ignore him, while you reward any advances he may make with treats or a little calm petting. Don't make a fuss of him at this stage – it is important to keep matters low-key. If you have noisy, insensitive visitors, your dog will be happier in a bed or other comfy spot in another room – there is no point in confirming his prejudices about people!

In between visitors, you can build up his trust in you, and therefore in the world in general, by spending time on play and unrelated training exercises. Dogs who are very nervous often benefit from a plug-in pheromone diffuser (obtainable from vets and some pet stores), which releases a calming chemical undetectable to us but not to him. Once your dog is able to relax in the same room as your guests, ask them to offer him treats, quietly and gently.

Prevention: As above, socialisation in puppyhood is essential to enable dogs to learn how to cope with strange people and situations. During the first few weeks, supervise how visitors interact with your new puppy (or new rescue dog), and protect him from guests who don't understand dogs and may accidentally frighten him. His early experiences with new people and situations need to be as positive as possible – it's much easier to build up his confidence from the start than to try and restore it after he has lost it.

PROBLEMS WITH PEOPLE

DOGS AND CHILDREN

Dogs and children make a wonderful combination – so long as both are properly trained and supervised. Left to their own devices, they can teach other terrible habits or hurt each other quite badly. Brought up together sensibly, they can help to teach one another consideration, responsibility and good manners.

HOW DO INTRODUCE MY NEW BABY TO MY DOG?

Action: Start planning well before the baby's arrival. Obviously you need to take into account your dog's individual temperament, training and experience of life. If he has been something of a 'mummy's boy', start accustoming him to receiving less attention, alternating fun training sessions with quiet 'time out' periods when he is required to settle down while you are occupied. If he is very boisterous, work on calming him down with increased exercise and training. Tackle any behavioural problems, such as jumping up, which might endanger the baby, and brush up on basic training such as the 'Sit' and 'Down', as well as 'Leave it', which you will certainly need once he sets eyes on the baby's toys. Do make sure that he walks reliably on a slack lead, and if possible practise walking him alongside the pram well in advance. Introduce him to friends' babies so that he can get used to the sight, sound and smell, and install nursery gates early on to accustom him to having his access to some areas limited. This is also a good time to introduce him to a safe den or refuge where he can retire if he feels stressed, in readiness for the time when the baby starts crawling and the dog may well feel the need to remove himself out of reach.

When the baby arrives, gently introduce your dog to the new family member. Encourage him to sit and watch while you are engaged in looking after the baby, rewarding him for good behaviour with treats so that he associates the new arrival with pleasant times and does not feel excluded. If you shut him away while tending to the baby, he may well become jealous, and certainly will not have the chance to learn appropriate behaviour or to bond with the new arrival. Many dogs are disturbed by the unfamiliar sound of a baby crying, so reassure your pet when he hears this. Schedule regular quality time for him

▲ Dogs can be very protective towards children, but it is unfair to both to leave them unsupervised.

▶ *Puppies and children need to be watched constantly.*

on the floor, place the puppy among them and let him approach them, making sure they greet him gently and don't frighten him. With a very young child, hold his hand and show him how to stroke the puppy. Never allow rough handling, teasing or over-excited play. Children need to be shown how to pick up a puppy, with one hand under the chest and one under a bottom, so as not to cause pain or injury; very young children must not be allowed to try. Limit play sessions initially to quarter-hour periods two or three times a day so that your puppy doesn't become over-excited or over-tired. You will need to be on hand constantly to ensure that play doesn't get out of hand on either side. Remember that puppies use their mouths to explore their environment and investigate new acquaintances, and be ready to intervene so that the pup learns not to mouth his human playmates. Involving older children in the puppy's training will be beneficial to both, but don't let very young children confuse the pup by playing at training.

within the baby's timetable to prevent him from feeling jealous or neglected. Given the opportunity, most dogs will develop a good relationship with a baby, but never take this for granted. **Never leave your dog alone with your baby**, no matter how trustworthy he may be: it is unfair on both to take the risk.

HOW DO I INTRODUCE MY NEW PUPPY TO MY YOUNG CHILDREN?

Children love puppies, but need adult supervision to ensure that they don't love them to death! **Action:** Explain to the children beforehand that puppies are vulnerable, need gentle handling, quietness and lots of rest. Before the pup arrives, set up a suitable indoor pen or crate where he can be protected from too much attention and enjoy uninterrupted sleep. When he arrives, have the children sitting

▶ *Growing up together can be an enriching experience for both child and puppy.*

PROBLEMS WITH PEOPLE

MY DOG PLAYS TOO ROUGHLY WITH THE CHILDREN

Cause: Lack of appropriate adult supervision. Children and dogs don't know instinctively when a game is getting out of hand, and childish excitement can easily lead to canine over-excitement.

Action: This problem needs to be tackled promptly, before anyone is hurt. Your dog needs to learn self-control and appropriate behaviour; your children need to learn to avoid over-exciting him. As a first step, limit play sessions to no more than 15 minutes at a time, always fully supervised by you. Make sure your dog has enough exercise to burn off surplus physical energy, and spend time on obedience training (away from the children). Identify the main problem areas in his play behaviour (jumping up, mouthing, snatching, etc) and work on these responses in particular (*see appropriate pages*). Take your children's ages into consideration when teaching them how to play safely with the dog: very young children need close supervision at all times, and your dog needs to be protected from them just as much as they need to be protected from him. Don't let them scream, make

▶ *Games like tug-of-war cause your puppy to compete with children rather than attend to them, putting your child at risk.*

sudden movements, or grab at the dog, but concentrate on teaching them to be quiet and gentle.

Older children can play an active part in training the dog. Explain that they must avoid exciting him by screaming and running about wildly. Ban rough games, such as play-fighting or tug-of-war, and substitute games such as hide-and-seek or fetch which actually teach the dog, through play, to pay attention to cues. Help them to become more aware of canine body language so that they can recognise when he starts to become over-excited, and explain that they must respond by stopping play as soon as he misbehaves. Show them how to reward good behaviour with attention and how to act out 'sending him to Coventry' for rough play, such as nipping or jumping up, by shutting off eye contact, turning dramatically away and refusing to acknowledge him – most children love acting a part, and often do better than adults in this form of communication.

Prevention: Never allow dogs to play with children unsupervised until both dog and children have learned how to interact safely – and never allow young children to play with dogs unsupervised in any case.

MY CHILDREN PLAY TOO ROUGHLY WITH THE DOG

Cause: As above.
Action: Set firm rules for the children. They should be taught to respect his feelings and leave him alone when he is sleeping, eating, or doesn't want to play; never to tease him; to limit caresses

▲ *Children can be clumsy and so can big dogs, even if sweet-tempered, so be constantly on the watch.*

to what he actually enjoys (few dogs enjoy being hugged tightly and clumsily – gentle stroking is preferable). Point out that dogs don't like quick movements and high-pitched screams, so they should avoid running and screaming around him. If they want to play noisy, exciting games, take the dog out of their way. Never leave your dog with children without adult supervision. Ensure that the dog has a retreat where the children are not allowed to invade his privacy – a bed or crate in a quiet corner – and don't let children play in or near this area. **Prevention:** Explain to children before acquiring a dog that they will need to treat their new pet with respect and consideration.

MY DOG KNOCKS THE CHILDREN OVER

Cause: Big dogs can be clumsy, especially when young; and young dogs, like young children, tend to dash about without looking where they are going.

Action: At times when you know your dog is likely to be hurtling about (e.g. when he is excited at the prospect of a walk), keep the children out of his

▲ *A wobbly toddler and an excited dog racing about at top speed – not a good combination.*
◀ *Take care – children can hug a little too hard!*

way, and when young children are toddling about, keep the dog out of their way. Make sure your dog has enough exercise to use up his surplus energy: if he has no chance to dash about madly off-leash on a walk, he is more likely to be rushing about at home near the children. With an energetic dog and vulnerable young children, it is essential to spend time on training, teaching the dog to stay close to you when the children are around. **Prevention:** Supervise, exercise, and train.

PROBLEMS WITH PEOPLE

MY DOG STEALS THE CHILDREN'S TOYS

Cause: Puppies don't know the difference between permitted toys and toys that they are not allowed – and neither do adult dogs, unless they are taught.

Action: First of all, keep children's toys out of your dog's reach. Toys should be tidied away when not in use. If a young child is playing with toys on the floor, separate the dog from temptation with a puppy pen, crate or nursery gate or, even better, sit nearby with the dog on a leash out of reach of the toys and practise his 'Sit stay' or 'Down stay', whichever he is happier with. Make sure he knows the 'No' and 'Leave it' commands. Practise 'Leave it' with your dog on leash and a row of tempting items (toys, socks, slippers, etc.), rewarding him for compliance with a game with one of his own toys. Do make sure your dog has an interesting range of toys of his own to play with; if you have young children, it may be best not to give the dog soft toys, to avoid confusion with a child's favourite teddy. If the dog manages to seize a treasured toy, never make the mistake of running after him and rewarding him with an exciting chase game; instead, run away from him and do something exciting to distract him (e.g. running into the kitchen, opening the biscuit tin noisily and making a great performance of enjoying eating). Once he has learned 'No' and 'Leave it', you can simply tell him to drop the toy and find him a distraction. Never punish your dog for playing with a toy that is not his own, or he is likely to learn to carry stolen objects out of sight behind the sofa where he can destroy them in peace!

Prevention: Follow the above course of action from day one – and keep your dog well exercised and occupied to reduce his urge to find his own amusements.

MY DOG NIPS THE CHILDREN

Causes: Dog (especially young dogs) has not yet learned bite inhibition and is play-biting; dog considers children to be of lower status than he is and believes he is entitled to correct them as he would a puppy; herding breed attempts to round up children; hunting drive

◀ *Dogs nip each other's faces affectionately, so it isn't safe to let a child put her face this close to the jaws.*

and no parent should rely on the dog's good nature remaining unspoilt forever. However, it is also vital to re-train your dog. Enrol in a good training class or consult a behaviourist, and work on general training as well as seeking help with the specific problem.

Prevention: Supervise all child-dog interaction and step in immediately to correct teasing or over-stimulating behaviour by children, play-biting by puppy, etc. Never leave young children alone with a dog, no matter how much you trust him – it just isn't fair.

One puppy versus three excited children – take care.

leads dog to nip at running children; child pesters or torments dog; lack of appropriate adult supervision.

Breed notes: Highly reactive breeds (e.g. terriers) may tend to nip before they think. Herding breeds (e.g. collies, corgis) often have a strong working drive and will attempt to round up family members, other pets, etc., nipping ankles to head the children in the desired direction.

Action: Take this problem seriously – nips can easily escalate to serious bites. Stop your dog's interaction with children until you have successfully tackled the problem. If you have young children, separate him from them with a nursery gate. Supervise, supervise, supervise! Never allow your children to torment your dog – it is surprising how often parents will boast that their dog has a wonderful temperament because he puts up with the children climbing all over him or pulling his fur. No dog should have to 'put up with' being mistreated, no child should be permitted to get away with such bad behaviour –

MY DOG IS OVER-PROTECTIVE TOWARDS THE CHILDREN

Cause: Over-developed or misdirected guard instinct.

Breed notes: Guard breeds such as mastiffs are most prone to this kind of behaviour.

Action: It's tempting to be pleased if your dog wants to guard your children from outsiders, but this could lead to serious incidents – for example, the dog might threaten or attack visiting children if he misinterprets play between them and his own family. Seek professional help immediately, and do not allow the dog to come into contact with visitors when the children are around.

Prevention: Ensure that your dog is properly socialised with visitors from a young age, and watch out for the first signs of this behaviour to nip it in the bud.

PROBLEMS WITH PEOPLE

MY DOG IS SCARED OF CHILDREN

Causes: Dog was not socialised with children in early life – children move faster and more suddenly than adults and have higher, more penetrating voices, and a dog who is not familiar with them may regard them as a new, sinister species. Alternatively, dog has had unpleasant experiences with children in the past (being grabbed, poked or otherwise tormented).

Action: The key to teaching your dog confidence is to take matters slowly and start working at a safe distance – don't try to 'flood' him by forcing him up close to the object of his fear. Find a friend with sensible children and ask them to help. Start regular reward-based training sessions and, when the dog is confident with these, have the children present in the room, at the farthest possible distance, during training sessions, and ask them just to sit quietly and ignore the dog completely, not even looking at him. You in turn should act as if the children are not there, and hold a short

training session, keeping your tone and attitude as cheerful and matter-of-fact as possible - trying to reassure him will only reinforce his fear.

With very fearful dogs, use of a pheromone appeaser (*see p.73*) may help. It will probably take several sessions before your dog is able to relax in this situation, but once he is coping well you can gradually have the children coming nearer, talking in soft voices, moving a little, etc. When he is comfortable with this and you feel he is ready, provide the children with titbits and ask them to walk slowly past him and drop a treat in front of him. The next stage will be for them to offer him titbits directly, by which time he will be able to accept these particular children as friends. Now you need to move on to a wider range of well-behaved children – ask your young assistants to conscript sensible friends, or ask if your local training class has a children's group.

Prevention: Make sure your dog is properly socialised with children as well as adults in puppyhood; protect your dog from badly-behaved children.

Terriers can be highly reactive to loud noises.

MY DOG GROWLS AT THE CHILDREN

Cause: Your dog is warning the children that he is uncomfortable with something they are doing.

Action: Start listening to the dog and establish

◀ *The happy squeals of a small child can be loud enough to hurt a dog's ears and can worry a timid dog.*

Teach children how to hand over a titbit to the dog gently and patiently.

behaviour. If his tolerance of normal childish behaviour is low, it is time for some re-education, using positive reinforcement to teach him to associate the children's presence and activities with praise and rewards. Because the children's safety is paramount, it is advisable to consult a behaviourist or attend a training class where the trainer appreciates the nature of the problem. Never punish or scold your dog for growling at your child.

▶ *A snarl doesn't necessarily mean a vicious dog, but may be a polite (by dog standards) warning that he has had enough and wants to be left in peace.*

what he is complaining about. Perhaps a child is actively doing something wrong, such as pulling the dog's tail; more often a child is unaware of his transgression, not realising that he is disturbing the dog's sleep, playing too close within the dog's comfort zone, or approaching too near his dinner. Remember that a dog who is ill, in pain or simply growing old will be understandably less tolerant than a healthy dog – for example, if your dog is suffering from arthritis, a toddler leaning companionably against a sore hip joint may prompt a growl because he is unintentionally hurting the dog. It is your responsibility to teach the child how to treat the dog with due respect to ensure his own safety.

If the child is too young to understand, protect them both with a physical barrier, such as a nursery gate or a dog crate. However, you also need to look at the dog's

He is behaving well, by canine standards, in giving a vocal warning rather than snapping. If you discourage him from this, next time he may feel impelled to bite first.

Prevention: Supervise and protect both dog and children; ensure that your dog has a private retreat where he can get away from the children, teach your children how to behave around the dog, and pay attention to your dog's body language while he is in the children's presence.

PROBLEMS WITH PEOPLE

MY PUPPY NIPS MY HANDS

Cause: Normal puppy play – puppies need to learn that human skin is thinner than that of their littermates!

Action: When your puppy nips, over-react! Squeal as if in pain, turn away from him nursing the nipped hand loudly, and halt play immediately. This is how his littermates would react if he used his teeth a bit too hard in a game, and it is how he will come to learn bite inhibition. React this way even if his teeth only touch your skin lightly to make sure the lesson goes home. Ensure that everybody who plays with him follows the same rules, especially children. Left to their own devices, children can easily over-excite a puppy and encourage him to nip, but if you enlist them in your 'teeth training' campaign they can often be better than adults at acting hurt and changing the game to 'playing statues' as soon as he uses his teeth. Be sure to provide suitable toys on which your pup can exercise his teeth as he wishes.

Prevention: Teach gentle behaviour consistently from the start to avoid problems later.

◀ Supervise puppies with young children to avoid nipped fingers.

however careful, should be stopped to prevent any risk of accidents; others believe that it is beneficial for a dog to learn self-control in always using his jaws gently and with consideration. You will have to decide which view you take. It can be a very endearing gesture; on the whole, however, this habit is best discouraged if your dog is going to be playing with children, who could be frightened or could jerk away suddenly, catching themselves on a tooth. To teach your dog not to mouth, use the same approach as with nipping.

Prevention: Don't let the habit start – squeal and withdraw the first time he tries it.

MY DOG NIPS PEOPLE'S FEET AND ANKLES

Causes: Excitement; fear of feet; herding behaviour.

▶ Children may encourage a puppy to nip playfully at feet and trousers as a game, leading to problems later.

MY DOG MOUTHS HANDS AND CLOTHING

Cause: Some dogs, even when they have learned not to use their teeth on human skin, like to use their mouths to gently hold people's hands or clothes.

Breed notes: Gentle mouthing is common among gundog breeds in particular.

Action: Some trainers hold that mouthing,

Breed notes: Herding breeds such as corgis and collies often have an inbuilt 'heeling' drive, nipping at feet and ankles to drive their 'flock'.

Action: Treat as with hand-nippers (*above*) by squealing and breaking off interaction. With persistent ankle-biters, applying a taste deterrent to trouser hems and shoes can also help. Dogs who are scared of feet (perhaps a rescue dog who has been kicked) need their confidence building up in all areas with patient, consistent reward-based training: once they feel safe, they will no longer need to defend themselves against imagined threats. If you have a herding breed, you may need to find him some other means of using his working drive, such as agility.

Prevention: Don't let the habit start – squeal and withdraw the first time he tries it.

MY DOG INSISTS ON LICKING HANDS AND FACES

Causes: Affection; insecurity; attention-seeking; comfort behaviour; expression of submission; dog is attracted to the taste of your skin, face-cream, body lotion, etc.

Action: Act as with nippers (*above*) by squealing and turning away. You can also use a taste deterrent such as lemon. However, you don't want your dog to stop showing you affection. You may decide that you are happy for your dog to lick, say, the back of your hand, but not your face, in which case you can offer your hand for a lick, praise him, and withdraw when you have had enough.

Otherwise teach your dog an alternative method of expressing affection, such as shaking hands or rolling over to have his tummy rubbed.

Prevention: Be clear and consistent in what you want your dog to do, and always withdraw if he starts licking when you don't want him to. Many people allow their dog to lick when he is a cute puppy, and then find themselves annoyed when their adult dog slurps a huge tongue across their faces – don't make this mistake!

▶ *Behaviour such as face-licking may be more acceptable in a Chihuahua than in a Great Dane!*

PROBLEMS WITH PEOPLE

AGGRESSION

Threatened or actual aggression towards humans is a problem that won't go away if ignored, and is likely to become worse. Because it has a range of causes, owners often misinterpret canine aggression (e.g. mistaking fear for protectiveness), so consulting a behaviourist should be your first step.

FEAR-BASED AGGRESSION

Causes: Lack of socialisation; previous ill-treatment; inherited timidity. Dogs who are scared of people often display aggression as self-defence. A dog who snarls at strangers from behind your ankles probably isn't being protective of his owner, simply afraid.

Action/Prevention: Puppies need to be properly socialised, meeting a range of people in safe, supervised sessions. Explain to friends, visitors and people you meet in the park that they should let your puppy approach them in his own time and be gentle with him. Don't let children treat him like a toy or tease him, don't expose him suddenly to huge noisy gatherings, and don't let well-meaning admirers terrify him by swooping on him from a great height. If his early experiences of humans are good, your dog is likely to grow up liking people. Unsocialised adult dogs need to start from scratch, learning to trust

▶ *Unsocialised dogs are distressed in company, as well as dangerous.*

people, but this is a long slow process and, because of the real risk that someone may be bitten, you are advised to seek professional help from a behaviourist. Fear-biters often don't give the same warning signals as more confident dogs, so consider using a muzzle when in public places.

TERRITORIAL AGGRESSION

Cause: Territorial instinct combined with inadequate socialisation.

Action/Prevention: Puppy socialisation should teach youngsters that humans are allowed to enter their territory. This doesn't necessarily reduce their value as home guards – most dogs will easily learn the difference between an invited guest and a burglar breaking into the house at night – but it prevents such problems as postmen being reluctant to deliver to your house and reduces the risk of visitors being bitten. If you have an adult dog who shows aggression towards visitors, it is essential to take precautions to protect people. Set up nursery gates to block his access to the front door and to rooms where you may invite someone in; ensure that your garden is dog-proofed, not only to keep your pet in but to stop trespassing children climbing over the fence; use a house line and tie your dog to a secure hook in the wall *(above)* before answering the door; and, above all, seek professional help from a behaviourist. Most overly keen guard dogs can be re-educated with time, care and sensitivity – simply shutting a snarling, scrabbling dog away every time anyone calls simply makes the situation worse.

DOMINANCE AGGRESSION

Cause: Naturally dominant dog; over-indulged dog. If your dog considers himself of higher status than some (or indeed all) humans, he will feel entitled to correct any human behaviour he disapproves of with a snap or a snarl.

Action/Prevention: Reduce your dog's opportunities to bully you by avoiding provoking situations – if he snarls when you hug him or when you roll over in bed, don't hug him, and shut him out of the bedroom. Start an organised training programme (you'll find this easier if you join a good training class) and establish your own higher rank in his eyes by making him work for all privileges. Over-assertive male dogs can often become more laid-back after neutering: consult your vet.

▲ Territorial aggression must be controlled and suitably directed to protect visitors.

OTHER FORMS OF AGGRESSION

Possessive Aggression: Some dogs are possessive of toys, rawhide chews, a favourite place to sit, etc. The simplest answer is to remove the object, and provide some substitute activity. Put toys away after games, stop buying chews, or block access to the seat, and spend more time in exercise, interactive games and training. A happily tired dog is less likely to feel argumentative about possessions!

Illness/Injury: A dog who is ill or in pain may bite, so handle invalids with care and, if a normally good-natured dog becomes uncharacteristically snappy, ask the vet to check him over.

Arguments over food may arise in multi-dog homes.

Food: Some dogs may be aggressive over food, often because they have at some time in their lives had to guard this valuable resource. The old-fashioned advice that dog owners should establish dominance by practising removing their dog's foodbowl while he was eating often led to increased food aggression! You can defuse this situation by teaching your dog that you are the source of food and not a threat: toss a few treats near or into his bowl while he is eating, reward him with titbits for good behaviour, and he will learn.

PROBLEMS WITH PEOPLE

MY DOG GROWLS AT THE CHILDREN

Cause: The dog is stressed by the children's behaviour, and is warning them to stop before he reaches his bite threshold.

Action: Congratulate yourself on having a good-natured dog (he is warning, not biting), and then give yourself a black mark for failing to supervise child-canine interactions adequately. Few children know instinctively what behaviour is safe and acceptable around dogs; they need to be taught, watched, and reminded. Very young children do not understand the difference between toys and living animals, and should always be supervised.

Even with well-behaved children, nervous dogs may feel stressed by their high-pitched voices and rapid movements. If you have exploratory toddlers or boisterous older children, your dog needs a refuge where he can retire for peace and safety. Regard growls as an invaluable early-warning system to enable you to take action before serious problems arise. Scolding (or punishing) a dog for growling at a child will simply add to his negative feelings about children. Instead, separate the dog and child, and later on make a point of involving them in a positive experience together, rewarding the dog with treats and a cuddle for being in the child's presence.

▶ *Children and dogs can be best friends.*

MY DOG GROWLS OR SNAPS WHEN I CORRECT HIM

Causes: Canine-human communication problem, e.g. dog has not understood what you are trying to teach; dog considers itself of higher status than owner; owner is employing inappropriate form of 'correction'.

▶ *Using force to train your dog often encourages him to argue in canine style, with growls or even teeth.*

Action: First identify the misbehaviour that leads you to correct your dog, and make it harder for the dog to carry this out. (If he chews your possessions, put items out of reach, use nursery gates to limit where he can go, and increase supervision; if he refuses to come out from under the table, temporarily block his access with cardboard boxes, etc.) Then review your method of correction. A confrontational approach is likely to put a dog on the defensive, especially if he does not understand why you are acting in what he sees as an aggressive manner. Instead, follow the route of ignoring and distracting.

When undesirable behaviour is directed at you (e.g. jumping up, pawing), make a point of ignoring your dog: turn away, shut off eye contact, and put on a great act of pretending he isn't there. Once he is settled, call him and set him some simple task, such as a Sit, which he can be

rewarded for – demonstrating that this action is rewarding, whereas the previous one wasn't. When misbehaviour is aimed at an object (e.g. chewing a shoe, scratching the door), go for distraction – ignoring the dog, start up an attractive activity on your own, such as tossing a favourite ball in the air, stacking cheese cubes on a plate, etc. When he comes to investigate, invite him to join in – much more fun than solitary destruction.

Increasing exercise and training sessions will also help your dog to focus more clearly on the idea that pleasing you is rewarding.

Prevention: Avoid confrontational, coercive correction.

MY DOG IS OVER-PROTECTIVE OF ME

Causes: Inadequate socialisation; dog allowed to assume high ranking, coupled with possessiveness towards owner; owner rewarding this behaviour. In many cases an apparently protective dog is simply frightened of strangers.

Action: If you have a dog who won't let people near you, stop fooling yourself! Your dog isn't protective – he's ill-mannered. This may be because he is scared of people and has discovered that snarling and growling drives them away, or it may be that he has too high an opinion of his rank and is simply

▶ *A good training class helps with socialisation.*

being bossy. Owners often reinforce this behaviour by sending out mixed signals, telling the dog to behave while feeling reassured by his 'protection'. Work on socialisation, and also on control: your dog needs to know that he cannot dictate who is allowed to approach you. It will help to attend a good training class, and to introduce house rules so that your dog has to work for rewards.

Prevention: Good puppy socialisation and consistent training.

▶ *Guard breeds are often intelligent and responsive companions, but it is vital to harness their guard instincts positively.*

MY DOG LACKS GUARD INSTINCTS

Causes: Breed with low guard drive; immaturity; well-socialised dog who has not yet needed to display guard instincts.

Action: Don't worry! Strong guard instincts are inappropriate in a companion dog, and most gentle family pets will respond suitably if there is a real threat. If you have chosen a guard breed, don't expect adult behaviour from a puppy: a well-balanced youngster shouldn't display guard behaviour early on.

Prevention: If you really want a guard dog, choose an appropriate breed, and ensure that his guard instincts are controlled by adequate training, .

PROBLEMS WITH PEOPLE

MY DOG IS AGGRESSIVE TOWARDS MY PARTNER

Causes: Rescue dogs with an unhappy history may have inbuilt difficulties with people of your partner's gender or appearance (e.g. distrusting bearded men) which can take time to overcome. Other causes: dog allowed to assume high ranking, coupled with possessiveness towards owner; dog picks up tensions between partners; aggressive behaviour has proved rewarding (dog receives attention). It's easy to be amused when a dog (especially a little one) favours one member of the household at the expense of another, but if not dealt with promptly this problem can soon get out of control.

Action: It's time to teach your dog his place in the household! This doesn't mean neglecting him or bullying him, simply instituting clear house rules so that he has to work for rewards instead of receiving them automatically. Teach him to sit for meals, not to barge ahead of you through doorways, to wait for an invitation before joining you on the sofa, etc. Don't punish or scold aggressive behaviour, but ensure that it is never rewarded – don't try to soothe your dog, and don't ever let him get away with growling, nipping, chasing or taking over your partner's chair. Use a house line to check him every time he shows aggression towards your partner, and remove him quietly from the scene without speaking to him or making eye contact.

For positive reinforcement, you need to co-opt your partner to work with you and establish that he or she is also a source of rewards. Ask your partner to take over feeding the dog some of his meals and to participate in reward-based training sessions. You will need to work together and be consistent in how you react to both desirable and undesirable behaviour. If the dog's aggression is serious, it is recommended that you consult a behaviourist to advise the safest way to tackle the situation.

Prevention: Establish consistent house rules from day one, and ensure that both you and your partner stick to them.

MY DOG IS JEALOUS OF MY PARTNER

Causes: Dog allowed to assume high ranking, coupled with possessiveness towards owner.

Action: Dogs who leap around barking, jumping and trying to barge in when their owners show each other any affection may seem amusing at first, but soon become a nuisance – and this behaviour can escalate into open aggression. It's important that your dog learns that his actions are unrewarding, so as soon as he reacts in this way, take him by the collar and lead him out of the room, without speaking or making eye

◀ *Asking your dog to sit for his meal teaches him self-control and good manners.*

contact, and shut him out until he is quiet. Make a point of greeting your partner before the dog and continuing to show your partner affection; but also schedule time for the dog to have his share of fuss to make it clear that there is room for all three of you in the household. As above, you also need to set firm house rules in place and make him work for rewards so that he recognises that he does not actually rank above your partner, and your partner should make a point of interacting with the dog in a positive way.

Prevention: When introducing a new partner into your home, pave the way for a peaceful

◀ *Don't let your dog come between you and your partner, for his sake as well as your own.*

relationship by taking your dog's needs into account. Minimise the disruption to his life by sticking to your regular routine of walks, meal-times, etc., and be sure to allocate time every day for play and training, both to reassure him that he still has his place in your life and also to reinforce good behaviour. Your new partner needs to spend time with the dog, too, to establish that he or she is now also a member of the family. It often happens that a new partner has different ideas about how a dog should be treated, so be sure to discuss what both of you expect of the dog at the beginning to avoid confusion.

▼ *A family dog needs to be involved with all the family, not just one member.*

MY DOG WILL ONLY OBEY ONE MEMBER OF THE FAMILY

Causes: Dog considers himself of higher rank than the other family members, other family members are inconsistent or confusing in giving commands.
Action: Members of the family who are having problems with the dog need to schedule regular reward-based training sessions, and may find it helpful to attend a good class with the dog. Young children should not be allowed to order the dog around, as they are likely to have difficulty with consistency and may have unrealistic expectations.
Prevention: All family members should be involved in the dog's training.

WILFUL ON WALKS

Walking the dog should be a pleasure for both dog and owner, but it's not uncommon to encounter difficulties. Quite a few dogs raise problems before even leaving the house, usually because either they are afraid to go out or they are over-enthusiastic at the prospect – polar opposites in terms of reaction, but equally frustrating to cope with.

MY DOG GOES MAD WHEN I FETCH HIS LEAD

Cause: Over-excitement and lack of training.
Action: Set aside a period of time before the walk, fetch the collar and lead as if you were about to take your dog out but, as soon as he starts bouncing and shrieking, simply ignore him and put the lead away. Continue to ignore him until he quietens down, then repeat the process. You may have to persist for a long time before your dog finally settles enough to have his lead clipped on in a calm and sensible fashion, and you will probably have to repeat the exercise for several days. An alternative approach is to put on the collar and lead and simply stay in with the dog, ignoring his excitement, then remove the lead after half an hour. With repetition, he will stop

▶ A walk should be pleasurable for the owner as well as for the dog – good manners matter!

associating the lead with going for a walk, but it is important to keep an eye on him during the time he wears it in the house to ensure that he does not catch his lead up on furniture and hurt himself. Whichever method you choose, it will help if you start working on the 'Sit' exercise, using reward-based training, so that you can tell him to sit while you attach his lead. Most dogs will be happy and excited when they realise a walk is forthcoming, but you will both enjoy the walk more if you can start out with good behaviour.

Prevention: Teach the 'Sit' and 'Stand' exercises early on, and accustom your dog to sitting or standing quite still while you put his lead on.

A dog should sit quietly while his lead is clipped on.

MY DOG WON'T WALK PAST A CERTAIN POINT

Causes: Pain/discomfort when walking (e.g. arthritis, sore paws); fear of something in the vicinity; dominance issue.

Action: Try to establish the reason for this behaviour. If walking causes your dog pain, this needs attending to. However, very often it is a mental obstacle that is the problem. With small dogs, it is simple to carry the dog *(below)* some distance and encourage him to walk home, or to pick him up at the stopping point, carry him a few yards beyond it and then resume the walk. With larger dogs, it is necessary to redirect their attention. Sometimes simply asking someone else to walk the dog a few times can change the pattern of behaviour. Otherwise, you need to focus the dog more on you and less on the area where he is walking, using a toy or food treats as above.

MY DOG IS RELUCTANT TO LEAVE THE HOUSE

Causes: Lack of early socialisation; fear arising from a past incident; physical illness.

Action: Once you have checked that your dog is physically sound, you need to build up his confidence. Schedule extra time for short, fun training periods in which you can focus the dog's interest on a favourite toy or food treat. Once he is keen on his reward, drive or carry him a short distance from home and then walk him back – going home will be more attractive to him than going away from home. En route, keep his attention on you rather than the walk with titbits or his toy. Repeat this exercise, sticking to the same route but gradually increasing the distance, until he is confident about it, and finally try starting from home.

Prevention: Make sure that walks are fun and rewarding for the dog. It's easy for a young, inexperienced dog to become scared of the various things he sees on walks, or for an older dog to become bored by the prospect of yet another dreary trudge round the block.

WILFUL ON WALKS

DOGS AND CARS

Difficulties can also arise before the walk begins if you have to drive to reach your favourite park or countryside walk and have a dog who is less than happy to be travelling with you in the car. Canine misbehaviour in cars is a real road hazard, and is potentially very dangerous. It often takes time and patience to reconcile a troubled dog to being driven around in a car.

think will attract his attention. If he shows any interest, toss him a treat and then go on ignoring him. Each advance from him should be rewarded. (You may wish to take a book with you, because this can be a long process.) Don't attempt to entice him into the car: the first step is to have him happily coming up to you while you are sitting in it.

Next, move further into the car so that he needs to reach his head inside to accept a treat; then to put his paws up on the seat, and eventually to jump happily into and out of the stationary car for a fuss. Don't rush things. Only when your dog is quite comfortable in the car should you move on to sitting with him in the car with the door closed, then with the engine running, and finally taking a short trip to somewhere rewarding like the park. Praise your dog lavishly for each advance, and ignore his nervousness – comforting him will only reward his negative behaviour.

MY DOG WON'T GET IN THE CAR

Causes: Physical discomfort/disability; lack of training; fear (anticipation of travel sickness; previous negative experience, as major as being involved in a car accident or as minor as experiencing car rides to the vet).

Action: If your dog has physical difficulty climbing in or out of the car, provide a step or ramp. If the problem is one of fear or anxiety, spend time making the car a happy place to be. Begin with a stationary car, settle yourself in one of the seats with the door open and your feet on the ground, ignore your dog and start playing with a toy, eating a snack, juggling dog biscuits or whatever you

▶ *A ramp enables an old, stiff or clumsy dog to climb in and out of the car with ease. Ramps come in various designs – look for a non-slip surface and ease of loading and unloading.*

▲ *Time spent before travelling building up good associations with the car is never wasted.*

Prevention: Introduce the car as a fun place to be early on in your dog's life. Remember that puppies (like human children) are more prone to motion sickness than adults, and that a puppy's first experience of car travel is likely to be stressful since it usually means leaving home for the first time, so do spend time providing positive car experiences.

MY DOG BARKS AND HOWLS IN THE CAR

Causes: Over-excitement; distress.
Action: This habit needs tackling as a matter of urgency: it is not just annoying but potentially dangerous, as it is liable to affect the driver's concentration. Try to find a helper to ride in the car and concentrate on the dog while you drive. The helper should stay very calm and quiet (shouting at a noisy dog is counter-productive, as he will think his humans are joining in!), but be quick with a soft 'No', and a gentle tap on the muzzle when the dog starts barking. It is often the

sight of movement out of the car window that sets dogs barking, so it may help to settle your dog on the car floor where his view is limited. Alternatively, if your dog is used to a crate at home, settle him in a crate in the car and if necessary cover it with a light sheet.

▶ *Dogs who bark and howl in the car may distract the driver and so cause road accidents.*

Dogs who are stressed by car journeys often react well to the use of a pheromone spray (available from your vet), which broadcasts a synthetic version of the soothing chemical produced by a dog's mother when he was a puppy and helps to calm him down.
Prevention: Make sure you have a helper with you on early car journeys to keep your dog soothed and well-behaved so that this habit never develops.

▲ *An assistant to supervise the dogs from the back seat while you drive is invaluable in the early days.*

WILFUL ON WALKS

MY DOG IS CAR-SICK

Causes: Stress; motion sickness.

Action: First, reduce your own problems by covering the car seats and carpets on the floor with protective sheets or towels and packing plenty of towels for mopping up! If your dog is tense and stressed in the car, he needs reassuring that the car is a safe and pleasant place to be (*see p.92 My dog won't get in the car*).

A technique which is very effective with nervous travellers is to take your dog for a very short drive (five minutes is enough) every day, with a rewarding experience such as a walk or a game at the end of each mini-trip. Then increase the distance slightly each week. A pheromone appeaser (*see p.92*) sprayed in the car to help him relax may assist.

▲ *Ventilation matters, but travelling with his head out of the car window puts a dog at risk.*

◀ *Car sickness is distressing for dogs as well as causing mess.*

For dogs who suffer from genuine motion sickness, there are a number of approaches to try. Don't feed your dog anything for three or four hours before a journey, give him ample opportunity for toileting before setting off, ensure that the car is well ventilated, and drive slowly and as smoothly as possible. Don't forget to schedule plenty of comfort stops on the drive. Some dogs respond well to a dose of glucose in water before travelling (this can be squirted into your dog's mouth with a syringe to ensure that he swallows the dose). His position in the car may make a difference: some dogs are less likely to be sick if they ride in the front seat (wearing a car harness for safety's sake), where they can follow the direction in which they are travelling, while others are more comfortable on the floor where they can't see the scenery flashing by. If necessary, you can ask your vet to prescribe medication for travel sickness.

Prevention: Accustom your dog to car journeys gradually from an early age.

MY DOG LEAPS ABOUT WHILE I'M DRIVING

Causes: Over-excitement and lack of training.

Action: A dog who dashes about the car is an accident asking to happen, so take action immediately to restrain your pet. The two basic

▶ *A canine seatbelt harness not only ensures that your dog sits quietly in the car, but protects him if there is an accident.*

options are a canine seatbelt harness or a crate, whichever your dog finds more comfortable. However, if your dog is behaving like this, it suggests that you need to spend time training him to behave appropriately, working towards a reliable 'Down-Stay'. Dogs often don't associate commands they know with different places, so once your dog has learned the 'Down-Stay' at home and out on walks you will need to practise it in the car. Start with the car parked in a quiet street, then move on to parking where there are more distractions, and finally enlist the help of a passenger to continue this training in the car while you drive. Even with the best-trained dog, though, it makes sense to use a physical restraint in the car simply to ensure his safety if you should be involved in a car accident or even if you have to brake suddenly.

Prevention: Always use a car harness or crate when driving.

MY DOG GUARDS THE CAR OBSESSIVELY

Causes: High territorial guarding instinct; fear-based aggression.

Breed notes: Guard breeds, such as German Shepherds and Rottweilers, need appropriate training to prevent their guarding drive from being misdirected.

Action: This is a problem that needs to be taken seriously and nipped in the bud – you may be telling yourself that the dog is protecting your property from car thieves, but he is far more likely to bite an innocent petrol attendant than a criminal. Re-educating your dog to prevent him from being a danger to the public requires a lot of time, patience and some dog-wise assistants, but, as with most aggression-based problems, the safest solution is to consult a canine behaviourist who will assess the individual circumstances of the case.

Prevention: Early socialisation of puppies is essential to ensure that they can accept the place of non-family humans in their world.

▼ *A well-trained guard dog doesn't need to be actively aggressive to deter car thieves.*

WILFUL ON WALKS

MY DOG PULLS ON THE LEAD

Cause: Failure of leash training.

Action: First, you may need to change the type of collar you use. Choke chains and other collars designed to cause discomfort when the dog pulls are unnecessary, don't work except in the hands of experts, and can cause permanent injury to your dog's neck and throat. Dogs don't think like people. If pulling on the lead brings pain or discomfort, most dogs don't reason that the action of pulling is responsible but tend to pull harder to try and escape from the pain. With toy breeds, a comfortable soft rolled leather collar is usually sufficient, and a gentle tweak with one finger on the leash, repeated every time the dog pulls the leash tight, is often all that is needed. With big powerful dogs a halter-style headcollar or a

special harness designed to prevent pulling gives the owner more control and removes the risk of exerting pressure on the dog's neck and throat. A headcollar gives you control of the dog's head to steer him into position without giving him the option to pull. It is important to obtain the right model and size for your dog's head shape, to ensure comfort and security, and also to spend time at home allowing your dog to become accustomed to the new sensation before taking him out in it.

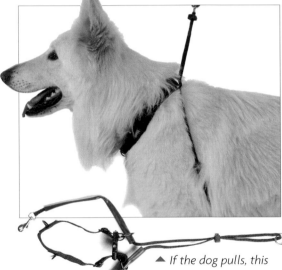

◀ *A dog who pulls on the lead may damage his throat – as well as your back. This is a habit that should be discouraged.*

▲ *If the dog pulls, this corrective harness creates an uncomfortable pressure under his front 'armpits'.*

An anti-pull harness works by putting the strain on the dog's forelegs instead of his shoulders, so that he cannot tug forwards effectively. Having ensured your dog's physical comfort and increased your own level of control, the next step is to re-educate him about walking on a slack lead. Keeping the lead fairly short, set off – and the moment he pulls, stop. Stand still and ignore him until he calms down, stops tugging and starts looking at you. Once the lead is slack and you have his attention, praise him and set off again. Repeat this behaviour as often as necessary.

Prevention: Never allow your dog to start pulling. From the first outing, respond to pulling by stopping or changing direction, while rewarding good behaviour with praise and treats.

A treat bag attached to your belt is practical.

◀ *Encourage your dog to walk to heel with verbal praise and treats: don't yank him into position with a tug on the lead.*

MY DOG WON'T WALK TO HEEL

Cause: Failure of training; inherent dislike of this position (some dogs are natural heelers, but the majority are not).

Action: Consider why you want your dog to walk to heel. The Border Collie-style 'wrap-around' heel position is required for formal obedience work, but has no particular advantage in ordinary life other than to demonstrate how well-trained your dog is. It demands close attention and good co-ordination from the owner, otherwise you may trip over your dog or accidentally kick him. For most pet-owners, therefore, training the dog to walk on a slack lead is easier and more practical – if you want him to walk close to you, simply shorten the lead. If, however, you do require a formal heel position, start by guiding your dog into place by your thigh by directing his eyes to a treat held in front of you. When he walks a couple of paces beside you in the right position, praise him and give him the treat. Once he has

the idea, introduce the 'Heel' command, using the leash to bring him gently back into position when necessary. You can couple this with a gesture such as slapping your thigh to bring him up to his place. Make sure your dog is happy heeling in a straight line before you introduce changes of direction, indicating each turn with a verbal and/or hand signal.

Prevention: From the start of leash training, keeping your dog's attention focused on you while he is on the leash should be a priority. Talk to him, carry a toy or treats, and make sure that responsiveness is rewarded. The leash is a tool of communication, like a horse's reins, and should never be used to drag (or be dragged by) the dog.

◀ *Slapping your hand on your thigh provides a visual and an auditory cue to remind your dog either to fall back or to draw forward into position.*

97

WILFUL ON WALKS

MY DOG IGNORES ME WHEN OFF-LEAD

Cause: Time off-leash is full of interest – free running, exciting scents, new people and dogs to meet. You've got a lot of competition for your dog's attention! Indeed, if you've been leaving him to his own devices while you stroll through the park, you've actually taught him to ignore you in favour of finding his own amusements.

Action: It's time to start competing for your dog's interest. Take his favourite toy to the park and invite him to play; take a pocketful of titbits and urge him to earn them through short, fun training sessions; play chase games and hide-and-seek; draw your dog's attention to points of interest, and let him show you what attracts him. In short, aim to be a companion rather than a mere escort, and your dog will do the same.

Prevention: Don't ignore your dog when he is off-lead!

▼ *Take a toy to the park. While he is playing with you, he is also learning to focus attention on you.*

▲ *Dogs love to run. Make sure your dog learns that running to you is even more fun than running off.*

MY DOG WON'T COME BACK WHEN OFF-LEAD

Cause: Failure of training. One common mistake is to take your dog to the park, let him off the lead to enjoy himself, then call him in to put his lead back on and march him home – almost certainly before he is ready to leave. What this teaches him is that coming to your call means an end to his fun. Another easily made mistake is to call him when he is engaged with something and reluctant to leave it. He doesn't come, and he learns that he doesn't have to come.

Action: Teach the recall from scratch, initially at home or in the garden. Start by offering a titbit at close range, stepping back a little and encouraging your dog to come to you. Give him the titbit, praise him for coming, and repeat. Once he has the idea, introduce the 'Come' command and keep

practising, gradually increasing the distance. Always reward him for coming, never scold him for a less than prompt response, and, in these early stages, never make the mistake of training when there are any distractions. When the lesson has been learned at home, take him to the park on an extending leash, let him have a good run around, then call him. If he fails to respond, call again and gently reel him in on the leash, praising him when he reaches you. Repeat this a few times and then continue the walk or have a game with him so that he does not associate the recall with the end of his fun time.

When you feel ready to practise off-leash, follow the same pattern – call him, praise and reward him for coming, and release him. Do choose your moment for calling. At this stage it would be setting up for failure to recall him when he is engaged with a playmate or a fascinating scent. If he doesn't respond, don't keep shouting or scold him – attract his attention with a high-pitched squeaky call and, as soon as he looks up, run away from him. Few dogs will be able to resist running after you and, when he catches up with you, you can praise and reward as usual. Build up the exercise slowly, and eventually you will have a dog who responds to your call no matter what he is doing.

Prevention: Start teaching the recall when your dog is still a baby and eager for your attention. On walks, call him to you several times for a fuss and then let him run off again, so that he doesn't associate the recall with the end of the walk. No matter how well your puppy has learned this exercise, don't be disappointed if he regresses when he hits adolescence – if you keep practising, he will revert to good behaviour as he matures.

▲ *Scent-marking is part of the joy of a walk to your dog, but he needs to learn when to refrain.*

MY DOG STOPS TO COCK HIS LEG ON EVERY TREE

Cause: Territorial marking, concerned less with emptying his bladder than with leaving his scent-mark on every way-post.

Action: Practise steady walking on the leash, gently tweaking your dog back into line when he veers off towards a tree or lamp-post. Off-leash, work on your recalls. Don't forget that your dog does need to cock his leg quite a few times on a walk, however.

Prevention: Train your dog to walk with you rather than doing his own thing. Castrated dogs urinate less often, so castration (coupled with training) will reduce this problem.

WILFUL ON WALKS

AGGRESSION ON WALKS

Dogs who lunge or snarl at passers-by and other dogs are an embarrassment, a social liability and a possible danger – and they are also dogs who are not getting or giving the enjoyment that a walk should provide. We label such behaviour 'aggression', but there is often more fear than fierceness underlying this reaction.

◀ Aggressive dogs need help to enable them to socialise normally, and safely.

MY DOG IS AGGRESSIVE TOWARDS OTHER PEOPLE ON WALKS

Causes: Lack of socialisation with humans at an early age; usually aggression is fear-based; occasionally inappropriately displayed guarding drive; rescue dogs may have cause to distrust strangers; a dog who is ill or in pain may snap at people who approach him.

Action: This is a serious problem, and it is advisable to consult an experienced trainer. Your first step should be to protect passers-by. A headcollar will give you more control over your dog than a standard collar (but ensure that it is correctly fitted, both for the dog's comfort and for security). If there is a real danger that your dog might carry through an attack, you may need to use a muzzle (again the fit is important: a basket muzzle is recommended, to enable your dog to pant and drink while wearing it). Next you need to establish the cause of your dog's aggression to find the best way to tackle it – whether the lesson he needs to learn is that people won't hurt him, or that he doesn't need to guard you, or simply that you are in control of the situation. Whatever the cause, you will need to work on focusing his attention on you, using

◀ A head-collar, properly fitted, gives the owner increased control.

▲ If you know your dog may bite, protect other people by using a muzzle when you walk him.

treats, toys and fuss, initially without distractions and then gradually with the assistance of friends who are prepared to act as stooges.

However, because this is such a serious problem, it is best to attend a good training class – or private lessons if your dog is genuinely dangerous.

Prevention: Good socialisation in puppyhood is essential to teach puppies how to feel comfortable with other people.

▲ Canine-aggressive dogs are a liability on walks and miss out on a great deal of enjoyment. It takes time and patience to re-educate them.

MY DOG IS AGGRESSIVE TOWARDS OTHER DOGS ON WALKS

Causes: Lack of canine socialisation at any early age; negative experience (being attacked or frightened by another dog); over-developed sense of dominance; adolescents (as with humans!) often develop bad manners which, if not tackled, can lead to a full-blown aggressive attitude; if your dog suddenly becomes dog-aggressive without apparent cause, there may be a medical problem. It is not uncommon for dogs who can handle off-leash social encounters with other dogs to be dog-aggressive when on-leash, because the constraint of the leash puts them on the defensive.

Breed notes: Some guard breeds (e.g. Akita), breeds with fighting-dog ancestry (e.g. Bull Terrier) and the feistier terrier breeds need intensive and sensitive puppyhood socialisation to prevent them from becoming dog-aggressive as adults.

Action: As above, start by preventing your dog from carrying out an attack by adopting a headcollar to increase your control over him, and if necessary using a muzzle when he is off-leash. The next important step is to focus the dog's attention on you while you are out. Walk him on leash, if possible in areas where you are least likely to encounter other dogs, and practise training exercises as you go along, rewarding every response with praise and a treat and encouraging eye contact. The more focused your dog is upon you, the less attention he has to spare for other dogs. Only when you have established this focus should you turn your attention to teaching your dog how to socialise with other canines. This is best done by consulting a behaviourist who uses positive reinforcement to re-educate problem dogs. Alternatively a good training class can help: you will need to discuss your dog's problem with the trainer beforehand to ensure that the class is appropriate, as you don't want your dog to upset or injure his class-mates, and negative experiences will only reinforce his attitude.

Prevention: Puppies need to have plenty of positive experiences with other dogs to learn how to interact appropriately.

WILFUL ON WALKS

MY DOG IS OBSESSED WITH FOLLOWING SCENTS

Causes: Scent-oriented breed; lack of alternative 'hobby'.

Breed notes: Expect this problem with breeds designed to follow scents – notably scenthounds and gundogs.

▲ *Bred for centuries to follow their noses, scenthounds are hard to dissuade from this habit.*

Action: Keep your dog on leash in areas of high temptation, and work on his recall. This is going to be a long, slow process. Start by taking him to an area where exciting scents are minimal, and walk him on a long line (10m/30ft), regularly calling him back, using the line to draw him gently to you if he does not come, and praising him

▲ ▶ *A long line is an invaluable aid when training, as it prevents your dog from developing the problem habit of running off and doing his own thing.*

lavishly when he reaches you. When he is coming reliably, move on to a higher-temptation area with more distracting scents, and repeat. At the same time, work on improving his focus on you, using fun, reward-based training with toys and treats, so that you can offer real competition to those exciting scents. Encourage him to become really enthusiastic about a favourite toy which you can take on walks and play exciting games with. If you can excite his interest in retrieving the toy (on a long line), move on to playing hide-and-seek with it, initially 'hiding' it within clear view and gradually making the hunt harder, so that he can enjoy using his scent abilities in an approved way.

Prevention: Make sure the first time your dog goes off after a scent is the last – once he discovers the joys of heading off on his own and realises that you can't stop him, the task of retraining becomes much harder, so follow up straightaway with a long leash and lots of training.

MY DOG GOES OFF WITH OTHER DOGS

Cause: Dogs are sociable creatures, and the other dogs are currently more interesting than you are!

Action: You need to become more interesting to your dog than his canine social life, offering him games and challenges and stepping up obedience training, with particular attention to the recall (*as above*). A good training class will speed matters up, as he will have to learn how to focus on you in the presence of other dogs. The trainer will be able to show you how to teach your dog an 'off duty' signal that means he is free to go and play with other dogs, as opposed to letting him make the decision.

Prevention: Ensure that puppy socialisation takes place within

throw the ball too far so that he is brought up with a jolt at the end of the line). As soon as he reaches the ball, tell him 'Bring it' in a happy, excited tone of voice, and gently reel him in towards you. If he drops the ball en route, try a little verbal encouragement, but if he fails to pick it up simply call him to you (using the line if necessary), walk over to the ball with him beside

▲ Dogs benefit from the chance to play with other dogs – but it must be on your terms, not theirs.

a structure, rather than a non-stop bout of puppy play without owner participation, so that your dog learns that other dogs are fun sometimes, but not the most important factor on outings.

▲ Ball games are more fun for both of you when your dog has learned to bring back his ball.

you on a short lead, and drop the ball into your pocket. Try again ten minutes later. If he does bring the ball back, give him lots of praise and hold your hand out for it. He may hand it over, or drop it on the ground for you to pick up, but if he has been in the habit of refusing to give it back he will probably hang on to it. In this case, ignore him. Stay where you are, keeping him on a short lead, and act as if he doesn't exist. Eventually he will abandon his treasure (it may take quite a while the first time round). Pick it up, praise him as if he had handed it over voluntarily, and start the game again. Repeat until he has the idea.

MY DOG WON'T GIVE ME BACK HIS BALL

Causes: Sometimes a dog simply hasn't made the connection between returning the ball to you and the continuation of the game; others have simply learned that it is more fun to hang on to the ball and get you to chase them.

Action: Have your dog on a long line (10m/30ft) when you throw the ball (but make sure you don't

Prevention: When playing ball, use the 'ignore' technique to make it clear that the game ends if he doesn't co-operate – never chase after him or grab at the ball.

WILFUL ON WALKS

MY DOG IS SCARED OF OTHER DOGS ON WALKS

Causes: Inadequate canine socialisation; bad experience with other dogs.

Action: Your dog needs a series of gradual introductions to calm, non-threatening dogs. If you rely on chance meetings with other dogs in the park or on the street, there is always a risk of encountering a boisterous or aggressive dog who will merely reinforce your pet's fears, so you need to seek out suitable company *(left)*. Contact local training clubs, looking for trainers who take a gentle, reward-based approach, and ask if they are able to help. Alternatively, you may have friends with gentle, friendly dogs whom you can arrange to meet on walks, avoiding hours when too many other dogs are around.

When another dog appears on the scene, make sure that you yourself present an appearance of relaxation and confidence. If you tense up in expectation of a worrying encounter, the tension passes down the lead and confirms your dog's stress, so don't tighten the leash or try to reassure your dog. Carrying treats or a favourite toy to distract and reward your dog in the presence of other canines will also help. It will take time, patience and many non-frightening encounters before your dog starts to relax, but it is worth the effort.

Prevention: Make sure your puppy is appropriately socialised with other dogs

OTHER DOGS SEEM TO PICK ON MY DOG

Causes: Inadequate canine socialisation may mean that your dog doesn't read canine body language and sends out the wrong signals; some dogs seem to carry a 'victim' scent which encourages aggressive dogs to attack; and, sadly, you may live in an area where there is a high proportion of irresponsible dog owners with aggressive dogs.

Action: Increasing your dog's socialisation time with friendly dogs will help him to handle canine encounters better, so treat as above.

Prevention: Early socialisation teaches canine social skills and reduces the risk of victimisation.

WHAT SHOULD I DO IF MY DOG IS ATTACKED BY ANOTHER DOG?

Action: If you see the attack coming, you may be able to deflect or repel the aggressor. It's not advisable to pick your dog up, which is unlikely

▼ *Inter-canine aggression can be frightening, but try to keep calm and avoid putting yourself at risk.*

support himself on his forelegs alone – but wait until their jaws are disengaged before pulling the dogs apart to avoid causing worse injury. You can then loop a leash around the aggressor's loins (so that it acts like a choke chain) and tie him to a fence or tree, so that you can attend to your own dog. If one of the dogs has a tight hold on the other and will not release him, you may be able to loosen his grip by wedging a stick (long enough to keep your hand safe) into his mouth from the side.

to halt the attack and simply puts you at risk. You may be able to put an aggressive dog off his stride with verbal aggression of your own (stamp your foot, step forward and shout, 'Go home!'); if you have one, opening an umbrella suddenly towards his face is often effective. Avoid looking the aggressor directly in the eye, as this represents a direct challenge in canine language. Once an attack begins and the dogs are engaged, don't try to separate them by hand, as you are very likely to be bitten. Shoving a solid object, such as a briefcase, between the two dogs may separate them long enough for you to drive the other dog off; tossing a coat over the head of the aggressor may also work; and, if you have access to a hosepipe or other source of water, you may be able to break the fight up this way.

Prevention: You can reduce the likelihood of an attack by learning to read the body language of approaching dogs. If you see a dog approaching with a stiff, tense posture, erect ears, rigid tail and a steady stare, it's time to change direction as casually as possible, taking care not to send out warning signals to your dog (such as tightening the leash). In areas where you are likely to meet aggressive dogs, it may be wise to carry a suitable repellent – probably the most effective is the trusty umbrella, which you can open with a whoosh to startle the oncoming dog.

If a helper is to hand, you can each try to grab a pair of hindlegs (keeping well clear of both dogs' heads) and lift these off the ground so that each dog is forced to

▲ *Learn to read the body language of approaching dogs. A polite approach like this is easily distinguished from an aggressive attitude, and is likely to result in a friendly encounter.*

WILFUL ON WALKS

MY DOG PESTERS OTHER DOGS TO PLAY

Cause: Inadequate/inappropriate early socialisation with other dogs – your dog has learned to enjoy canine play as a puppy, but has not progressed to learning good adult manners, so he expects every dog he sees to be his playmate.

Action: Dogs who dash wildly up to every canine they meet, however well-intentioned, can frighten timid dogs (and owners) and run the risk of provoking a fight with aggressive dogs, so this problem needs to be tackled. Until he has learned sensible manners, walk your dog on an extending leash so you can check this behaviour *(below)*,

perhaps using a headcollar so you can turn his head away from other dogs. Make sure that he has enough physical exercise – walks, play and training sessions – to use up his surplus energy. Schedule several short training sessions every day to focus his interest on you and increase your control over him, working in particular on the recall. Mix play with training, and stop intermittently during games to ask him to sit for a treat before resuming play.

When he has become more responsive, walk him in the park on an extending lead to practise calling him back from other dogs. If possible, seek out a training class where the trainer appreciates his problem and is prepared to spend time socialising him with calm, sensible dogs who will teach him that they don't have to play if they don't feel like it.

Prevention: Make sure that your puppy attends a good puppy socialisation class where he will learn that there is a time to play with other dogs and a time to listen to you. Being allowed to socialise with every dog he meets in the class, or attending poorly run classes where the 'pupils' simply run around having a good time, won't teach him sensible behaviour. On walks, remember that you should supervise your dog when he is off-lead – he should not be allowed to do just as he likes and run up to every dog he sees. Call him back to you every now and then for a fuss or a food treat, so that he finds you more interesting than other distractions.

MY DOG PESTERS OTHER PEOPLE IN THE PARK

Causes: Dog likes people and is insufficiently focused on owner. Often this problem is caused unwittingly by dog-loving strangers (and indeed friends) who make a fuss of your adorable new puppy, leading him to expect everyone to welcome his attentions.

Action: Congratulate yourself on having a dog who is people-friendly – now work on having a dog with good manners! As with dogs who pester other dogs *(above)*, keeping your dog well exercised and putting effort into general training forms the first step, and dealing with the specific problem comes second. Once your dog is paying

◀ Dogs need to know how to interact politely with other people.

more attention to you and is responsive to the Recall and 'Leave it' commands, you can ask some friends to meet you in the park (ideally early in the morning when few other people are out) and act as stooges, splitting up to cross your path at intervals during the walk. Have your dog on an extending leash, and as each person approaches, call him back to you. If he ignores you and dashes up to them anyway, they should ignore him completely, and if necessary you can check him slightly with the extending lead to prevent him from actually making contact with them. Repeat this with each friend you meet.

When he does pay attention to you and comes to you when called, praise him and give him a few food treats. Keep practising this until he has learned not to rush up to everyone he meets. Once he is steady, you need to teach him to differentiate between people who want to make contact with him and those who don't. Ask him to sit when you meet people, and teach him to hold his position quietly unless they invite him to approach, when you should give him the command, 'Say hello', and let him advance. People who want to greet him should be asked to reward him for remaining calm by petting him or giving him a treat, but to shut off eye contact and turn away sharply if he tries to bounce at them.

Prevention: A good puppy socialisation class is the first step towards learning manners, backed up by constant supervision when your dog is off leash so that he does not have the chance to develop bad habits.

▼ Don't let your dog spoil other people's walks by pestering their dogs to come and play.

WILFUL ON WALKS

MY DOG WON'T RETURN TO THE CAR AFTER HIS WALK

Causes: Dog is not ready to come home yet, wanting more exercise, more socialising or just more fun (energetic, young dogs can be like children who don't want to go home from a party); car may have negative associations.

Action: If negative associations surrounding the car are the main problem, see p.92 (*My dog won't get in the car*). If your dog just doesn't want to end his walk, reconsider your walk schedule. Is he getting enough exercise? A good walk with some off-leash running should leave a dog happy to curl up in the car for a nap, so lengthening your walks

▲ *After a satisfying walk, most dogs are happy to climb into the car for a well-earned rest.*

or tiring him out with ball games may solve the problem. Does he enjoy enough of a social life? If meeting other dogs on a walk is a rare treat, join up with a local dog-walkers' group or enrol in a training class. Providing regular chances to mix with canine friends will reduce his need to stay with other dogs after his walk.

If you are satisfied that he has enough exercise and enough canine company, it may be that going home feels dull and unstimulating after the fun of

a walk and you need to make the return trip more inviting. Make a big fuss of him in the car before driving off, provide a post-walk treat (a chew or food-stuffed toy) to entice him back into the car and enjoy on the way home, and give him a regular play session as soon as you get back so that he has something to look forward to. If you combine more exercise, more social life and more fun after the walk, most dogs will change their attitude to the trip home.

Prevention: Be aware of your dog's needs; try to be even more interesting to your dog than other competing attractions.

MY DOG IS SCARED WHEN WALKING IN TOWN

Causes: Many human country-dwellers feel the same! A crowded town is full of noises, strange smells, trampling feet, traffic, and stinky exhaust pipes right at a dog's nose level. With nervous or sound-sensitive dogs especially, it takes time and patience to build up confidence in such a situation, and dogs who have missed out on socialisation in puppyhood will find it much harder to adapt as adults.

Action: Treat your dog as an unsocialised puppy and build up his confidence gradually, walking only in quiet streets with low traffic until he is relaxed in this situation and working up – at his pace – to busier areas. An unsocialised dog of a sound-sensitive breed (e.g. a collie) may take months or even years to learn to cope with high volumes of street traffic.

▲ *It's amazing how well most town dogs cope with noise, smells and bustle – given a little help.*

Prevention: Expose puppies, gently and gradually, to as many strange situations and noises as possible, to help them cope with difficult situations in later life.

MY DOG WON'T WAIT OUTSIDE SHOPS

Causes: Dog has not been trained to stay; dog feels abandoned.

Action: Years ago, it was normal behaviour to take your dog to the shops and leave him outside while you did your shopping. In the 21st century, sadly, things have changed. Tied up outside a shop, your dog is at risk. He may be stolen, pulled about by children or attacked by another dog. He may learn inappropriate behaviour such as pestering passers-by. Most seriously, if harassed by strangers or other dogs, he could be put in a position where he feels forced to defend himself and snaps or even bites – whereupon you could end up in court and he could end up being put down as a 'dangerous dog'.

Ideally, therefore, one should never leave a dog outside a shop. If you absolutely have to, the answer is to work on the 'Stay' command (which is useful in many other circumstances in any case). Start at home in very gradual stages, building up from a three-second stay with you a few inches away from the dog to a one-minute stay with you out of sight, then practising away from home as well as gradually lengthening the time. Always reward a stay with praise and a treat. If he breaks the stay just take him back to the starting point and begin again – never scold him for not understanding what he is meant to do. Eventually he will have the confidence to stay where he is told until he Is released and rewarded.

Naturally you should also tether him securely by his lead to a solid hitching point, like a lamp-post or fence rail. Make sure that you leave some slack in the lead so that he can stand without feeling undue pressure on his collar and neck. Don't leave him on a long line or loose extending lead, however, as he might then roam into the path of passing pedestrians or even traffic.

Prevention: Avoid leaving your dog anywhere without your protection; teach the 'Stay' command as part of his regular training.

▼ *He's waiting patiently, but is he safe? Don't take risks with your dog if you can possibly avoid it.*

WILFUL ON WALKS

MY DOG IS SCARED OF PASSING TRAFFIC

Causes: Most puppies will naturally be scared at their first encounters with traffic because of the noise, size and speed, and need to be gently habituated to it. In adult dogs, the problem is usually due to lack of such habituation in earlier life; in some cases, an unpleasant experience involving vehicles may be to blame.

Breed notes: Herding breeds such as collies are often especially sound-sensitive and need careful introduction to noisy traffic.

▲ *Dogs brought up in rural areas with little traffic may well have problems adapting if they are asked to cope with the rushing cars of city life.*

Action: Reintroduce your dog to traffic from what he considers to be a safe distance. This might be a seat in the park set well back from the road, a quiet street with few cars, or even your own front garden, where he can see (and hear) traffic but it is far enough away not to be terrifying. Build up his confidence, and his focus on you, with plenty of games and reward-based training sessions, until he is completely ignoring the distant cars. From this stage, build up his proximity to traffic gradually. You may find a head-collar useful on walks, as this will enable you to guide his head away from scary distractions and back towards you – it will also provide extra control if you have a powerful dog who might bolt when frightened. Remember not to cuddle and reassure a frightened dog, as this will reinforce his fear, but make it clear that you, as leader, are relaxed and find nothing to worry about. If you have a friend with a sensible, confident dog, it can help to walk the two dogs together so that your dog can see that his canine companion remains calm.

It's not uncommon for a dog which is quite calm in ordinary traffic to be worried by one particular type of vehicle (refuse carts, road-sweepers, etc) – usually something especially noisy and/or not regularly encountered. The approach described above (gradual habituation from a distance) is just as appropriate for such cases, but you will have to seek out offending vehicles. If the refuse cart is the problem, schedule walks around the rubbish collection timetable, initially keeping well behind the vehicle and building up gradually to the point where your dog can walk alongside it without concern.

Prevention: Introduce puppies to light traffic early on – rather than wait until his vaccinations are completed, you can carry a young pup outside in your arms for short trips to accustom him to noise and bustle as early as possible. Don't flood your puppy immediately with too much experience at once: take him out when there is little traffic at first, and work up to noisier times. When your puppy is ready for walks, make sure that excursions among traffic lead to rewards (titbits, fuss, a game in the park) rather than letting them be simply bladder-emptying exercises.

▲ *Make sure your dog is confident walking on a quiet street with minimal passing traffic before you introduce him to busier roads.*

MY DOG BARKS AT PASSING TRAFFIC

Causes: Fear; desire to chase (hunting or herding drive); territorial drive.

Breed notes: Herding breeds such as collies, if not supplied with adequate outlets for their instincts, may react in undesirable fashion to anything that moves.

Action: Nervous dogs should be habituated to traffic as above. Frustrated hunters, herders and guards need a 'focus and distract' programme. Essentially you need to make yourself more interesting to your dog (as the source of games, treats, mental challenges, etc.) to focus his attention on you rather than whatever is passing by, and also to establish a reliable distraction (a titbit, a favourite toy) to cue him away from the undesired behaviour. If your dog is watching you, he isn't watching the traffic! Reward-based training is usually quicker and more effective than relying on physical deterrents, such as spray collars and rattle cans, which can in many cases make matters worse.

Prevention: Early exposure to everyday sights and sounds (at an appropriate level – don't start with a city centre rush-hour!) is the best preparation for teaching a dog to ignore traffic as an everyday matter. However, it's also important to ensure that your dog has enough going on in his life to satisfy any working instincts and use up surplus energy.

▲ *Urban dogs usually comes to take the sight and sound of traffic for granted, just as their owners do.*

WILFUL ON WALKS

CHASING PROBLEMS

Dogs are chasing animals who come with an inbuilt drive to run after anything that moves – whether as predators or in play. In some dogs (notably sighthounds and herding breeds) this instinct can be intense. However, it's an urge that has to be controlled, not only for the safety of other people and livestock, but also to keep your own dog out of danger near busy roads.

MY DOG CHASES JOGGERS

Causes: Playfulness; hunting drive; sometimes a dog who is actually afraid of strangers will feel the urge to chase them if he sees them apparently in retreat and running away.

Action: Take this problem seriously – even if your dog only wants to play. Joggers who don't understand dogs may be alarmed or distressed at being pursued. In areas where you are likely to encounter joggers, keep your dog on the lead, work on encouraging him to walk steadily beside you on a slack lead, and be prepared to deflect his attention to you and your pocketful of treats the moment a jogger appears. It may pay to practise the 'Sit' exercise as the jogger runs past, focusing your dog's attention on an enticing reward. When he is steady as people run past, move on to an extending lead and work on developing a good recall before you consider allowing him off-leash – any chance he gets to repeat this behaviour will undo much of

your hard work and necessitates starting from scratch again. It's always better to be able to call him back than to run after him, which will simply make him think you are joining in the chase – and he can almost certainly outrun you, anyway.

Prevention: Keep your dog's attention focused on you during walks, use the leash to keep him out of situations where it is easy to misbehave, and work on the recall exercise.

MY DOG CHASES CATS

Cause: Cats run, dogs chase – it's an inbuilt instinct.

Breed notes: Sighthounds, herding breeds and terriers have an extra-strong chasing instinct.

Action: Dogs rarely catch cats, so it's tempting to take this problem lightly. However, cat-chasing can be a dangerous hobby. In pursuit of a cat (or a squirrel, or other similar temptations), a dog might dash out into traffic and cause an accident, or might knock over a child or a fragile old person. Teach your dog not to chase small running creatures, using the same technique as outlined above, in order to protect him from causing or suffering an accident. Not all dogs can learn to overcome their chase instinct. If you have a dog with a strong prey drive, you may need to keep him on the leash in situations where he is likely to encounter temptation.

Prevention: As described above.

MY DOG CHASES SHEEP AND OTHER FARM LIVESTOCK

Causes: Play; hunting drive. Sheep panic easily and make such tempting targets as they run away!

Action: Be aware that sheep-chasing is a serious offence, and farmers are entitled to shoot dogs who chase their livestock. Considerable damage can be done by a dog chasing farm animals, even if he is 'only playing' and the animals appear unharmed – meat animals lose hard-won condition when stressed, and pregnant beasts may abort their young. Five minutes' fun for a dog can mean bankruptcy for a farmer! If you live in the country, do spend time walking your dog on leash near livestock and teaching him to ignore them. However, whether your dog encounters farmstock on a daily basis or only on annual holiday in the country, and whether he is well-trained or not, the golden rule is to keep him on the leash near farm animals. It's an act of courtesy towards the farmer whose land you are on or near, and a safety precaution to ensure that your dog cannot even be suspected of a crime which carries for him a possible death penalty.

Prevention: Train your dog, but always use a leash near livestock.

MY DOG CHASES TRAFFIC

Causes: Play; chase instinct; territorial instinct.

Breed notes: Collies and other breeds with a strong herding instinct seem to be particularly prone to traffic-chasing.

▲ *These dogs are at risk! Duck-chasers may get into difficulties and drown, while cattle-chasers may be kicked by a cow or shot by its owner.*

Action: For his own safety and that of motorists, keep your dog away from traffic. He should be indoors, in a securely fenced garden or on a leash in areas where there is traffic – although obviously this is going to be difficult if you live on a farm or other large property where the incidence of traffic is occasional and unpredictable. As well as seeking to contain the problem, you need to work on teaching a reliable recall and keeping your dog busy so that he has no surplus energy to waste on undesirable activities.

Prevention: Physical containment; plenty of training.

WILFUL ON WALKS

DOES MY DOG NEED A COAT IN WINTER?

It depends on your dog's natural coat. Thick-furred huskies cope happily without any artificial protection in Arctic conditions, while fine-coated Whippets shiver on a moderately cool day. If your dog has a thick soft undercoat, this will fluff up in the cold to trap warm air (acting like thermal underwear), and flattening the fur by putting a jacket on him will actually leave him feeling colder. If he has short fur with little undercoat, he will probably benefit from a warm, waterproof jacket — although if he is young and fit, he may well race around enough to keep himself naturally warm. Remember that very young, old or unwell dogs lose heat more easily and may appreciate a bit of extra help in keeping warm, while dogs living indoors in warm houses will feel the cold more than outdoor dogs. Damp is more of a danger than cold: dogs who are wet and chilly after a walk need drying off thoroughly afterwards, and in heavy rain a waterproof jacket will reduce the amount of wet fur you have to dry.

CAN MY DOG COPE WITH WALKS IN SNOW AND ICE?

Snow and ice shouldn't trouble your dog unless he is very young, old or infirm, so long as you take care to rub him down well after a walk, removing any ice and lumps of snow from his coat — long-haired dogs can build up hard-packed snowballs in their feathering. Pay particular attention to grooming in cold weather: fur needs to be clean and not matted to provide maximum insulation. If your dog is very active, he may need an increase in rations over the winter — keeping warm uses up a lot of energy.

Paws are a dog's most vulnerable point in icy conditions: compacted ice between the pads can leave them cracked and sore, while rock salt and other de-icers used to treat roads and pavements can burn the skin. To reduce the risk, keep your dog's toe-nails short in winter, trim the fur around his paws if he is long-coated and clip off any fur between his toe pads (use narrow-bladed scissors held flat against the foot to avoid the risk of cutting him) to reduce the amount of snow collecting between his toes. After walking in icy conditions, wash your dog's paws in warm water to dissolve ice and remove mud, rock salt or other de-icers from between the pads.

◀ *Compacted snow balled up in the fur is most easily removed by rinsing it off with a bowl of warm water.*

HOW DO I PROTECT MY DOG FROM HOT WEATHER?

Action: Hot weather is more hazardous for dogs than cold, so take care, especially if your pet is old or obese or has heart disease or breathing difficulties. Short-nosed breeds, such as Pugs, are particularly vulnerable. Never leave your dog in the car on a hot day – cars heat up fast to

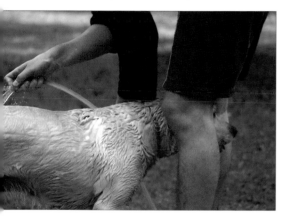

▲ *A hosepipe is a useful way of cooling down an overheated dog on a hot day.*

dangerous levels, even in the shade. Restrict summer walks to the cooler early morning and late evening, never in the full heat of the day. Remember that your dog's paws are sensitive, and hot pavements (or the floor in a concrete run) can burn his feet. If he is outside in the garden, ensure that shade is available. Dogs who enjoy sunbathing don't always have the sense to come out of the sun in time, so you may need to chivvy your pet into a cooler corner.

Make sure fresh water is always available. Always carry water on walks; at home, on really hot days, change your dog's water frequently and try dropping an ice cube in the bowl to keep it

cool longer. Good grooming is important in the heat. Clipping or shaving off a dog's coat isn't always the answer to hot conditions: the insulation of a well-groomed undercoat may keep your dog cooler than clipping – if in doubt, ask for guidance from a professional groomer.

Dogs are more vulnerable to heatstroke than humans because they don't have the cooling mechanism of sweating through their skin. Heatstroke can kill quite quickly, so watch out for symptoms – rapid breathing, heavy panting, salivating, stressed appearance, and frantic heartbeat or, in the later stages, collapse and coma – and take action immediately if necessary. Remove the dog to a cool, well-ventilated area and, if possible, immerse him in cool (not cold) water to bring down his temperature. If you can't do this, wet him down with a hose or other means. Offer water to drink, but don't try to force a drink down him as he may inhale it or choke. As soon as possible, seek veterinary assistance.

▲ *Make sure that shade is always available to your dog in hot weather, particularly in exposed places. Like children, dogs need supervision to ensure that they don't stay out in the sun too long.*

HORRIBLE AT HOME

Often the misbehaviour that bothers an owner is just part of a larger problem in that their dog lacks manners generally. You will probably need to look at your dog's bad habits in the context of his general conduct at home, rather than tackling one problem in isolation.

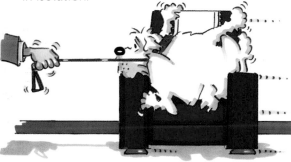

MY DOG IGNORES COMMANDS

Causes: Communication failure (dog does not understand what is required); owner inconsistency in giving commands; dog has learned that owner cannot enforce commands; dog may be deaf.

Action: You need to go right back to the beginning and start training your dog as if he were a new puppy. Often it can be helpful to join a training class to give yourself some direction and encouragement – but do check out the course first to be sure that you are happy with the approach and methods used. Remember also that a weekly class alone won't achieve very much: it needs to be followed through with daily training sessions at home. Because your dog needs to unlearn what he has learned so far (i.e. that commands can be ignored), avoid giving him any instructions unless you are in a position to (gently) enforce them. For example, leave a house-line trailing from his collar so that, if you want to tell him to get off the sofa, you can back up the 'Off' command by picking up the line and gently tugging him towards you.

Prevention: Train early, regularly and consistently so that disobedience cannot become a habit.

MY GOOD PUPPY HAS TURNED INTO A TEENAGE HOODLUM

Cause: When dogs hit adolescence (typically 8-18 months – later for larger breeds), hormonal changes prompt them to become more independent and more challenging. As with humans, some pass through adolescence without problems, but many go through a rebellious phase when they challenge authority, appear to have forgotten what they learned earlier, are easily distracted, and are more interested in exploring the world and developing a social life than in conforming to what the family wants. Some become over-confident and bumptious; others go through a 'spooky' stage when they find everyday objects or activities frightening.

Action: This may feel like the least rewarding period of dog-owning, but it is now that you need to make a heavy investment of time and effort. Be clear on what behaviour you want from your dog, be patient and consistent in your training, and as

far as possible try to avoid situations where bad behaviour is self-rewarding. Don't leave him unsupervised in the presence of temptation of any kind, whether the kitchen counter or the laundry basket; make sure he has enough exercise to use up his growing energy; and make training sessions fun to keep his interest. Remember that although his second teeth have probably come through now, they will be causing him discomfort and he will need approved (and appealing) chew toys to deflect his attention from items that you don't want him to chew.

Don't scold or punish bad behaviour, but if necessary treat your dog as if he were a baby puppy again and start from basics. During this period his learning capacity and ability to remember what he has learned will be at their lowest, but if you keep up the daily training sessions the effect will appear when he reaches maturity. If he displays seriously antisocial behaviour, such as overt aggression, consult an experienced trainer or behaviourist to help you, and him, solve this problem before it becomes

▲ Playtime is part of the learning process, encouraging your dog to focus on you and building up his confidence and responsiveness. Don't expect instant results though.

habitual. Make plenty of time for interactive play with him, introducing games where he has to concentrate (such as hiding a toy in the garden and encouraging him to find it) and providing plenty of motivation in the form of treats and favourite toys, so that your company is rewarding enough to compete with distractions. Keep up sensible, controlled socialisation with dogs and people, but avoid exposing him to scary situations at this stage, as fears learned now may stay with him all his life.

Prevention: Early neutering prevents many of the effects of adolescence; but many dog-lovers consider that it may also prevent a dog from developing full physical and mental maturity. Adopting an adult dog means you miss out on the 'terrible teens' period, but an older dog may be carrying emotional baggage which requires just as much effort to sort out. Not all dogs are difficult in adolescence – cross your fingers and hope!

◀ *▲ If you catch your hooligan dog in the act of destruction (left), interrupt him with a firm 'No', but scolding him after the event (above) won't help.*

HORRIBLE AT HOME

GRAPPLING WITH GROOMING

Grooming isn't just about hygiene and coat care: it's also an opportunity to carry out regular health checks, a means of bonding with your pet, and a method of reminding a bossy dog who is in charge. Unfortunately, if your dog hasn't had a good introduction to the process, he may be very unco-operative.

MY DOG WON'T LET ME BRUSH HIM

Causes: Negative experience (combing out tangles can hurt); dog considers himself of higher status than you (which is why many dogs who play up at home act like little angels at the grooming parlour, where staff make it clear kindly but firmly who is in charge); lack of training (dogs have to learn to stand or lie still without squirming, snapping, playing, etc.).
Action: Start with a dog who doesn't desperately need grooming: if your dog's coat is tangled, have him professionally groomed first to tackle all problem areas. Tether him on a

short lead, so that he can't run off (and, if he snaps when groomed, so his head end is secured). Place one hand under his belly, behind the ribs, so you can apply a soothing tummy-rub and also gently stop him sitting down. With the other hand, gently run a soft bristle-brush down his back, stroking rather than brushing and interspersing the strokes with calm hand caresses. Don't tell him off if he wriggles, snarls or acts up in any way; praise him if and when he does stand still. At this stage don't try to groom him, just to accustom him to the process. Repeat this every day, gradually increasing the brushing element to work towards the appropriate grooming for your dog's type of coat. Be very careful when tackling tangles and working on sensitive areas, to ensure that you never cause pain. Time spent on this exercise is never wasted: it makes it much easier to teach your dog good behaviour in other areas.
Prevention: Start daily short sessions with your new puppy, using a soft bristle brush, from day one. A puppy's coat doesn't need much grooming, but this is the time to establish the routine in his mind, well before you have tangles and mud to deal with.

MY DOG WON'T LET ME CLEAN HIS TEETH

Causes: Dog has not learned to allow you to handle his mouth; occasionally, a sore mouth (dental or gum infection) may be the problem.
Action: Stop trying to clean your dog's teeth and start teaching him to accept handling of his muzzle. Several

◀ *Teaching your dog to stand still to be groomed is a valuable lesson.*

times a day, when petting or grooming him, stroke his face, touching his muzzle and under his chin. Once he is happy with this, move on in gradual stages to touching his lips, lifting them slightly to show the teeth, touching the teeth, and rubbing your finger along the teeth. Next you can introduce the toothbrush, initially miming the cleaning action in between finger touches, and working up towards actually cleaning the teeth. Don't rush the process, but make sure he is happy with each stage before taking matters a little further. Eventually he will regard this as part of his daily routine.

Prevention: Start the above process with a new puppy right at the start, not attempting to clean his teeth but working towards a dog who is quite happy for you to handle his muzzle, open his mouth, touch his teeth and so forth.

MY DOG WON'T LET ME CLIP HIS CLAWS

Causes: Dog has not learned to allow you to handle his feet; dog has been hurt when claws were clipped inexpertly; many dogs have ticklish or sensitive paws; occasionally, sore paws (gravel rash, minor injury) may be the problem.

▲ Start handling paws in puppyhood so that this becomes an accepted routine, making it easy to check claws and clip as necessary.

◀ Lift your dog's lip gently at the side of the mouth to check teeth – don't force the jaws open.

Action: As above, start by teaching your dog to accept simple handling of the area. Start by stroking each paw in turn, and build up to holding them, gently working between the pads with your fingers, then holding individual claws; then introduce the nail clippers and spend a while miming the action of clipping to accustom your dog to the sound. Only when he is happy for you to hold a paw quite firmly and handle the claws, and is not worried by the presence of the clippers, should you try clipping. Be very careful not to cut too short – if you cut the quick, it will hurt, and it will bleed – and also take care not to pull on the claw.

Prevention: Start the above process with a new puppy right at the start, teaching him to be comfortable with having his paws handled.

HORRIBLE AT HOME

MY DOG SNATCHES TOYS

Cause: Dog has not been taught to take toys gently from your hand.

Action: To teach your dog to take objects gently, start by using treats. Show him an attractive titbit, close your hand into a fist around it and offer him the back of your fist. While he tries to take the treat by poking, pawing, licking or nibbling, keep your hand closed. Eventually frustration will cause him to back off a little. Reward any movement away from your hand by turning your hand over and offering the treat from your flat palm *(below)*. Repeat this simple exercise until

he gets the idea that grabbing doesn't work, but waiting politely does, and then introduce the commands 'Leave it' and 'Take it'. Now you can expand the exercise to apply to toys as well.

Prevention: Teach puppies from the start to treat human hands with care. Tackle rough play by yelping and withdrawing your hand the moment that teeth make contact with skin, and use the same technique to discourage snatching – if your puppy grabs something you are holding (unless you have specifically invited him to play in this way), squeal as if you are hurt and 'send him to Coventry' for a few minutes. Introducing the command 'Gently' early in puppyhood is also helpful.

MY DOG STEALS ITEMS TO PLAY WITH

Cause: It's fun! Until you teach him otherwise, any object is a potential toy to a playful youngster. Items with your scent on, such as dirty laundry, are particularly appealing.

Action: Until your dog has learned to respect your possessions, you will need to go through a spell of extreme tidiness. Putting everything tempting out of your dog's reach for a few months is a chore, but it will save your possessions, prevent your dog from establishing a bad habit, and provide a wonderful opportunity to instil tidiness in the family. Obviously tempting objects will sometimes be around (e.g. when children are playing with their toys), and at those times you should restrict your dog's access to the area with a nursery gate, or have him on a house-line and supervise his movements closely. Individual items can also be protected with a foul-tasting deterrent spray. At the same time, he needs to learn 'Leave it' *(see above)* and 'No'. In fact,

▼ A deterrent spray may help save your shoes from becoming chew-toys.

▶ *Tug-of-war is a fun game, but never let your dog tempt you into playing this with stolen items, or you reward theft!*

he needs daily training sessions in all the basic commands – the more you teach him, the more attention he will pay to you and your requirements.

Provide him with approved toys of his own, join in his play with them and praise him for using them. These should not include 'people toys' such as old slippers, which will make it harder for him to distinguish between your possessions and his own. Provide plenty of physical and mental stimulation for him so that he doesn't need to provide his own amusement. If he does steal an item, never chase after him (which he will see as a game) – try ignoring him, opening a packet of biscuits with as much rustling as possible, and eating one with much lip-smacking and obvious enjoyment!

Prevention: Supervise your puppy closely; limit his access to vulnerable treasures when you are unavailable for supervision; and teach the invaluable 'No' command (meaning, 'Whatever you are doing, stop it at once!') early on to employ whenever your pup approaches something he shouldn't have .

MY DOG WON'T GIVE BACK STOLEN ITEMS

Causes: Dog is seeking to initiate a rewarding chase game; dog considers himself higher-ranking than you and therefore entitled to retain items.

Action: Leave a house-line trailing from your dog's collar. When he picks up something he shouldn't have, put your foot on the line to stop him running off, tell him 'No!' and draw him gently to you. Pretend complete disinterest in the stolen object, but put him into a Sit beside you, keeping the lead short, and keep putting him back into the Sit position as necessary but otherwise ignoring him. In this position he can't play with his new toy, and will eventually drop it – at which point you use the leash to prevent him from grabbing it again, and praise him lavishly for dropping it, offering a treat reward and immediately leading on to some other activity to distract him. Keep the atmosphere low-key and neutral so he has no temptation to challenge you and become argumentative. With repetition, the lesson will sink in.

Prevention: Never reward theft with any kind of excitement (particularly not the chase game). Teach your dog that stealing things is boring (the long sit without interaction), whereas playing with his own toys is fun.

◀ *Children's toys are often an irresistible temptation to a dog, so make sure they aren't left lying around to be chewed by an untrained puppy.*

HORRIBLE AT HOME

POSSESSIVE GUARDING

Guarding any resource, from a favourite toy to your own bed, by growling or even snapping when people approach, is a habit that needs to be nipped in the bud – not by scolding or punishment, which confirm the need to guard, but by proving that you are the source of good things rather than a potential threat.

▲ A dog who feels he has to guard his space is not just a nuisance – he is stressed and unhappy. Teaching him manners will make him more relaxed.

MY DOG GROWLS WHEN WE APPROACH HIS BED

Cause: Resource guarding; dog may not have been allowed to enjoy his bed in peace.
Action: Ensure that all family members respect your dog's right to a quiet zone and don't disturb him in his bed. Now you need to teach your dog to respect your right to walk about in your own home without being snarled at. The best way to do this is to teach him to welcome your approach. Start by walking past his bed with a food treat, initially keeping outside the distance at which he will start snarling, and, without pausing or meeting

▶ Nobody wants a dog who shows aggression in the home, and a dog whose growls are ignored may go on to bite. This problem needs tackling.

his eyes, toss it to him while he is in his bed. Repeat this several times a day, approaching from different angles, offering different forms of treat, and reducing the distance only when he has started to relax, so that he comes to associate your approach to his bed with a pleasurable experience. Make haste slowly – if you rush things, he will only become more reactive.
Prevention: Site your dog's bed in a quiet area where he won't be disturbed; teach children to leave him alone when he is in his bed; and institute the treat-tossing routine immediately if he shows signs of guarding this area.

MY DOG GROWLS WHEN WE APPROACH HIS TOYS

Cause: Resource guarding; dog may have had toys taken away from him without (to him) apparent cause. (Don't confuse this behaviour with play-growls, which are meant to invite you to a game with the toy.)
Action: Avoid confrontation while your dog is playing with a toy by keeping outside his 'guarding zone'. Don't scold him or try to take his toy away,

which will make him more defensive. Instead, set up 'trading games': offer him a toy (not one of his favourites), then offer him a treat. As he drops the toy, give him the treat, praise him, and give him back the toy when he has eaten his titbit. With repetition, always ensuring that he is rewarded for giving up his toy to you, he will stop seeing you as a competitor. As he learns the routine, you can introduce the 'Drop it' and 'Take it' commands, which will be useful on many other occasions.

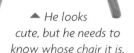

▲ *He looks cute, but he needs to know whose chair it is.*

Prevention: Practise 'trade-ups' from the early days, and never allow anyone to tease your dog with his toys.

MY DOG TAKES OVER A CHAIR AND WON'T GIVE IT UP

Cause: Your dog thinks he is higher-ranking than you and has a right to choose the best seat.
Action: First of all, stop his access to the chair – balance an upside-down dining chair on the seat, or lay a prickly upside-down carpet protector on it. Now you need to teach him to jump off chairs and sofas on command. Call him up on to a less favoured seat by patting it and showing him a treat. Don't reward him for getting up, but, before he can settle down and make himself comfortable, give him the 'Off' command in a happy, inviting voice, patting the floor and showing him the treat, and reward him with the treat and lots of praise as soon as he jumps down. (If he is

uncooperative, use a house-line to gently draw him off the seat.) Keep practising this, rewarding compliance with lots of fuss and praise and avoiding a confrontational approach, which will simply make him more aggressive over this issue.
Prevention: Teach 'On' and 'Off' at an early stage, and be consistent – don't let your dog start to develop a habit you don't want to become fixed.

MY DOG HAS TAKEN OVER OUR BED

Cause: As above.
Action: Ban your dog from the bedroom – sharing your bed is a privilege which you can award him and which you can take away if he doesn't deserve it. Put up a nursery gate so that he cannot enter the room. Make sure he has a comfortable bed elsewhere, and be prepared to start 'bed training' from scratch as for a puppy (*see p.124*).
Prevention: If you are happy for your dog to share your bed, make sure he understands that it is yours and that he may only join you upon invitation.

HORRIBLE AT HOME

WHERE SHOULD MY DOG SLEEP?

Your dog should sleep wherever you feel is the right place. Contrary to what some trainers say, sharing your bed won't automatically make him feel dominant, and sleeping in a crate in the kitchen won't make him feel rejected. What matters more than the site of his bed is establishing principles of bedtime behaviour. If you are happy for him to share your bed, avoid dominance issues (in case he turns out to be the bossy type) by ensuring that you get in first, then invite him to follow. Dogs find it natural to sleep with their pack; they can be comforting bedfellows and excellent hot water bottles. However, disadvantages of bed-sharing include dog hairs, muddy paws and occasional fleas; some

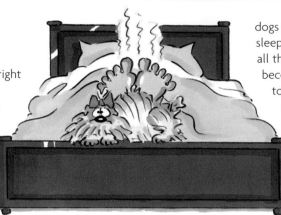

dogs fidget, while others may sleep like a log but tend to hog all the covers; clingy dogs may become clingier if encouraged to stay with you all night; and even a Chihuahua takes up a surprising amount of space (if you have a Great Dane, the bed-sharing option is not likely to be practical).

If you prefer your dog to sleep in his own bed or crate downstairs, be prepared to put time and effort into teaching him to settle down and sleep through the night without disturbing you. Make sure that his bed is big enough for comfort, warm enough in winter and cool enough in summer, and that his bedding is safe and washable. Baby puppies are best started off in a crate or pen (which should include toileting space to prevent them soiling their beds) in your bedroom, as they normally find it quite distressing to be alone at night for the first time in their lives; as they settle, you can move the pen in gradual stages to outside the bedroom door and eventually to your chosen site.

MY DOG WON'T SLEEP AT NIGHT

Causes: Insufficient physical and/or mental exercise during day; emotional insecurity; unsuitable bed or sleeping area; noises outside the house; late meal at night producing an energy surge at bedtime; urinary tract problems; puppies find it hard to adapt to sleeping alone after leaving their littermates; puppies and elderly dogs may not have enough bladder or bowel control to last through the night.

Action: Try increasing daytime exercise, including

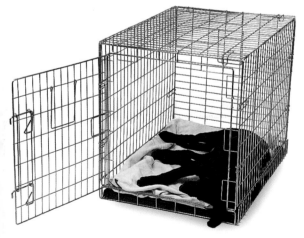

▲ *If you opt to use a crate, make sure your dog learns to regard this as a desirable den, not a prison cell, before shutting him in it.*

fun training sessions; schedule the evening meal earlier; and ensure that your dog has toileting opportunities just before bedtime. A veterinary check-up may be in order, especially with older dogs. If you regularly respond to the disturbance by going down and trying to settle your dog, he is likely to find this rewarding and will continue the behaviour; however, most owners find that this is one problem that doesn't go away if ignored. A compromise that is often successful (if there is no underlying physical cause) is to go down to your dog but ignore him, making yourself a cup of tea and sitting in the room with him without paying any attention, then retiring to bed again. This seems to provide reassurance without encouraging your dog to be a nuisance.

Prevention: Tired dogs sleep well. Keep your dog busy during the day, and you have a better chance of undisturbed nights.

◀ Most Bulldogs snore. However, heavier snoring may indicate breathing problems, needing veterinary attention.

on a slimming regime (less food, and a gradual increase in exercise). Sometimes a change of bed may help, giving the dog a chance to try different sleeping positions. See your vet if your dog has only recently started snoring or if he has other symptoms such as breathing difficulties, daytime tiredness, coughing or wheezing, nasal discharge, or bluish tongue or gums. However, in most cases dogs who snore aren't in the least bothered by it – you are the only sufferer! If it's a major problem, the answer is much the same as with a snoring spouse: sleep in separate rooms, or invest in earplugs.

Prevention: Keeping your pet fit and healthy may reduce the likelihood of this problem.

MY DOG SNORES

Causes: Obesity; allergies; head structure (short-muzzled breeds often snore); respiratory problems; polyps in the throat.

Breed notes: Short-muzzled breeds (e.g. Pekingese, Bulldogs) tend to snore because their elongated soft palates obstruct their throats.

Action: Check that your dog is not overweight: if he is, start him

▶ Every dog needs somewhere comfortable to sleep, away from draughts and other disturbances.

HORRIBLE AT HOME

PERSISTENT BARKING

Guard dogs who bark to sound the alarm have always been valued; but dogs who bark persistently for no good reason can drive owners (and their neighbours) mad. You need to work out why your dog is barking before you can tackle the problem: is he set off by some stimulus, or is lack of stimulus driving him crazy?

◀ Most owners want a dog to bark sometimes, so it pays to teach your dog to 'speak' on command.

MY DOG BARKS AT ME

Causes: Excitement; happiness – like children, some dogs just can't have fun quietly; attention-seeking; plain bad manners (i.e. lack of training).

Breed notes: Some breeds are noticeably more vocal than others, including most Spitzes, many terriers, and some guard breeds.

Action: Make this behaviour unrewarding by ignoring your dog when he barks. Don't just passively ignore him – he may not notice! You need to act out the message 'I am ignoring you' loud and clear: stop the game or the food preparation if this is what has set him off, shut off eye contact, turn away, and leave the room if necessary. Once your dog is quiet, return to him, give him a little low-key praise, and continue whatever activity set this off in the first place. Repeat as many times as necessary, and go on repeating on subsequent occasions for as long as it takes for your dog to get the message. It may take weeks, but remember that you are saving yourself years of irritating noise. It's much more effective than scolding him or trying to distract him, both of which reactions he will find rewarding (even the response of scolding, which counts as paying him attention).

Prevention: Make sure that you always respond to unnecessary barking by shutting off your attention. (Obviously there is such a thing as acceptable barking – you probably want your dog to alert you to danger or the doorbell, and to warn off intruders.)

MY DOG BARKS AT NIGHT

Causes: Boredom; loneliness; insufficient exercise/attention during daytime; toileting needs; disturbance by noises from outside.

◀ ▲ Repetitive barking releases endorphins ('feel-good' chemicals), so can become a comfort habit to reduce stress.

▼ *A new puppy needs to feel secure at bedtime to avoid later problems. A crate in the bedroom is a good start.*

Action: Getting up and going to attend to your dog's needs simply rewards his behaviour and makes it likely he will bark for you again the next night. Ignoring the noise, i.e. not rewarding it, may discourage him after a few nights; but, as the neighbours of persistent barkers know all too well, it may not. Positive action is preferable. Your dog is more likely to sleep through the night if he has had an interesting and active day, especially if you schedule a long walk or play session before bedtime to tire him out. If he is simply unhappy at being left alone, he may be comforted by a ticking clock or a radio left on the lowest volume, a night light (sited out of reach so he can't chew it) so he isn't left in the dark, or an appealing chew toy to keep him occupied. Consider whether there may be a physical cause (such as a urinary or gastric infection) for his restlessness, and consult the vet if necessary. If none of these helps, consider changing the dog's sleeping site. Does he have to sleep alone if he hates it that much? Could he sleep in a crate in the bedroom?

Prevention: A new puppy is going to cry in the night when he is left alone for the first time in his life – a crate in the bedroom is a better start, gradually moving this outside the bedroom and then downstairs if you wish. If he is in the same room as you, not only will he have the comfort of your presence, but you are to hand to discourage any whining or crying. One method is to keep a can of pebbles by the bed, which you can rattle to startle your puppy into quietness. Don't reward night noise with fuss and cuddles, but equally consider that this is a baby who should not be bullied.

HORRIBLE AT HOME

MY DOG BARKS WHEN I AM OUT

Causes: Boredom; loneliness; separation anxiety; guard instinct; disturbance from outside.

Action: Consider how long you are leaving your dog alone. If you are out all day, he can hardly be blamed for being bored and lonely. It isn't fair to leave a social animal alone for long periods, and you need to arrange for a dog-walker to call in or even consider rehoming him. However, a well-adjusted dog ought to be able to cope with shorter periods alone. Make sure he has a good long walk before you leave him, so that he is more likely to enjoy a peaceful rest; provide him with something to do in the form of a bone or a food-stuffed toy; and perhaps leave the radio playing softly to provide some form of company. For dogs who really can't cope with being home alone, treat for separation anxiety (*see pp.148-9*).

Some dogs are prompted to bark by noises from outside which may arouse their guard instincts or merely worry them. You may need to spend time while you are at home teaching your dog not to react to sounds such as dustbin collection or police helicopters. Settling him down in a back room away from the source of noises can help. It may even be that local children are deliberately provoking him while you are out by rattling the fence or banging on the windows, which is often a difficult problem to deal with, entailing contacting parents or local schools to explain the situation.

Prevention: Spend plenty of time on training, teaching your dog not to react to external

▶ *Barking is one of the commonest canine problems.*

▲ *It's important to establish why your dog is barking. Sometimes he may have a perfectly good reason to bark, from a canine point of view.*

stimuli by barking. Practise leaving him alone for very short periods from the start, gradually building up the time, and ask neighbours to report if he is barking.

MY DOG BARKS AT BIRDS AND SQUIRRELS IN THE GARDEN

Causes: Play/hunting drive; excitement.

Action: Break the habit by allowing the dog into the garden only when you are there, and spend time working on basic obedience exercises (including focusing your dog's attention on you and the recall) and play. This will not only increase your control over your dog, but use up his physical and mental energy – tired dogs aren't so keen to chase garden wildlife. You can supplement this approach by accustoming your dog to wearing a long line in the house, so that you can sit indoors with the door to the garden open and use the line to check him if he starts a noisy dash outside. Some dog-owners have found a solution in short term use of a spray collar, which squirts the offender with water or a strong-smelling chemical, such as citronella, whenever he barks, but this is not recommended for nervous dogs.

Prevention: Time spent interacting with your dog in the early days prevents bad habits from developing.

MY DOG BARKS AT PASSERS-BY

Causes: Excitement; boredom; guard/territorial instinct; nervousness.

Action: Have your dog on a long leash indoors, and arrange for a friend to act as a casual passer-by at regular intervals. Sit down and relax. When your dog starts barking, call him over in a soft voice, using the leash to draw him to you if necessary, and tell him, 'Quiet'. If he responds, reward him. If he keeps barking, repeat the command, still quietly, and hold his muzzle gently closed. Repeat each time your friend (or anyone else) passes by. Keep your own voice and reactions muted – shouting at your dog or trying to soothe him are both counter-productive and will encourage him to go on barking. Some dogs respond better to counter-conditioning with a sharp, unexpected noise – use training discs or a tin filled with pebbles or coins, and drop them abruptly when he starts barking. If this startles him into silence, call him over and reward him. Again, you will need to repeat the process several times. Whichever approach you choose, it will be more effective if backed up by spending more time on general training and fun. The more you can take your dog out and increase his socialisation, the less he will feel the need to over-react to external stimuli. You can also help by shutting him in a quiet room away from the sound of passers-by when you go out, drawing the curtains so that he cannot see out, and leaving a radio playing to muffle external sounds.

Prevention: Make sure that new puppies are gradually exposed to a range of sounds and sights that might stimulate them to bark, teach the 'Quiet' command early, and reward calm behaviour.

▲ *Leaving a radio playing when you go out can help to reduce loneliness as well as muffling worrying sounds from outdoors.*

HORRIBLE AT HOME

MY DOG IS HAND-SHY

Causes: Dog may have been smacked or slapped, or had his muzzle grabbed to stop him barking, and so consequently he sees hands as threats. Some naturally submissive dogs may cringe away from an approach simply out of excessive politeness.

▶ *Make sure that your dog associates your hands with positive interactions.*

Action: Stop all physical punishment. You now need to teach your dog that hands are a good thing, bearing titbits and caresses. Set up a routine of offering your dog a treat with one hand while gently touching him with the other. Initially, it will help if you make yourself as unthreatening as possible. Crouch or sit rather than looming over the dog, stay still and keep quiet, avoid eye contact, and offer the treat with your hand held low rather than overhead. Repeat this several times a day, for as many days as it takes. When your dog is confident with the process, build up to touching him just before you give the treat. Any time that he shies away or cringes, withdraw both hands and wait a few seconds before trying again. Building up confidence is a slow process (perhaps a couple of months), but it is worth persisting – a dog who is hand-shy may go on to snap at hands and perhaps injure someone.

Prevention: Keep your dog's experiences with hands positive – don't smack or grab him, but do regularly stroke and hand-feed titbits.

MY DOG IS SCARED OF LOUD NOISES (FIREWORKS, THUNDER, ETC.)

Causes: Sensitive hearing; dog picks up owner's fears; unpleasant past experience associated with loud noise.

Breed notes: Some breeds, e.g. German Shepherds and Collies, are especially prone to noise sensitivity.

Action: Make a 'den', enclosed on three sides and the top, where your pet can take refuge and feel secure. A big cardboard box will serve, set up in a quiet corner and made comfy with blankets, or you may be able to improve on an existing favourite bolt-hole. If your dog is happy using a crate, cover this with a blanket but leave the door open so that he can come and go as he chooses.

The next step is to change your own reaction to loud noises. Even if you don't like loud fireworks or thunder yourself, it is important to greet these noises with apparent pleasure and interest or even mild excitement ('Wow! That was a good one') in order to give the right cues. Your dog needs to know that you are completely unworried by the noises. Don't comfort or reassure him, as this will merely confirm that there is something to be afraid of; and certainly don't scold him, which will simply increase his negative associations. You can also reduce his stress by drawing the

curtains during storms or firework displays, turning the radio on quietly to muffle the noises, and using a pheromone diffuser, available from your vet.

Some noise-phobic dogs respond well to a desensitisation tape or CD (available from pet stores and some vets), which features sounds such as thunder and fireworks. This should be played initially at a volume low enough for your dog to disregard it,

▲ *Puppies need to get used to noisy household gadgets while they are still young.*

building up the volume in very gradual stages. It may also be worth contacting your vet to discuss medication that may be prescribed in anticipation of noisy events such as Bonfire Night.

Prevention: Puppies should be accustomed to a wide range of noises while they are still young. This doesn't mean filling their environment with a barrage of loud bangs, but making sure they hear everyday sounds – hairdryers, vacuum cleaners, the occasional door slamming – and learn to live with them. If you have a very quiet home, it may be beneficial to invest in a desensitisation tape which you can play (not too loudly) while your puppy enjoys a distracting game or you make a fuss of him.

▲ *A dog's ears are far more sensitive than ours; he may actually find the bangs of fireworks quite painful.*

Keep your dog indoors on Bonfire Night.

HORRIBLE AT HOME

MY DOG IS ALWAYS ESCAPING

Causes: In practical terms, the cause is your failure to make your home and garden secure to prevent escape. However, you should also look at the reasons why he feels the need to do so – most probably boredom, loneliness, fear, separation anxiety or, if your dog is a bitch in season or an uncastrated male, the urge to seek out a potential mate.

Breed notes: Some breeds, including most terriers and huskies, are addicted to escapology, and need extra-secure gardens.

Action: Check your dog's escape route: does he jump the fence, climb it, chew holes in it or dig

▲ *A determined dog can wriggle through a surprisingly small gap under a gate.*

under it, or has he mastered the catch on the gate? Making the garden escape-proof solves part of the problem: now you need to work on making your dog's life more interesting and finding appropriate uses for his energy so that he will be content to stay at home. If he is left alone for long periods, make sure he has a good walk before you leave him, provide him with a food-stuffed toy to keep

him busy, leave the radio on for company or, if possible, arrange for a dog-walker to take him out. If he suffers from separation anxiety, you will need to undertake a programme of confidence-building (*see pp.148-9*). With a dog who is impelled to escape when frightened by something beyond your control (such as thunder or fireworks), make sure he is secure before you go out, and in the long term work on desensitisation (*see p.130*). Increasing physical and mental exercise and spending more time with him in stimulating activities will deal with any excess energy and make you and your home more appealing to him. If your dog is not neutered, consider the operation, both to reduce his or her urge to roam and to avoid adding to the problems of canine over-population.

Prevention: Dog-proof your property before acquiring a dog.

TIPS ON DOG-PROOFING YOUR GARDEN

1 Staple chickenwire across any gaps in the fence.
2 To prevent digging under the fence, secure the ground in front of it by laying bricks or paving

▲ *Many dogs are good jumpers, so make sure fences are high enough to keep your dog in.*

MY DOG DASHES OUT OF THE FRONT DOOR WHEN I OPEN IT

Causes: Desire to escape (*see above*); lack of training.

Action: In the short term, shut your dog behind an inner door before opening the front door, or keep his collar on and affix his lead before answering the door. In the long term, however, you need to teach him to sit or go and lie down on an appointed spot when you go to the door. Initially, train without distractions; later, enlist friends and neighbours to ring the doorbell so you can practise answering the door.

Prevention: Never let a new dog or puppy have the opportunity to discover that he can nip through the door. Use a leash, an inner door, a dog-gate or a crate until you are absolutely certain he is door trained. Start door-training from day one, teaching him to sit and wait until the command to go out. Ensure that family and visitors don't undo your hard work.

stones, or attaching chickenwire to the base and sinking it at least 45cm (18in) into the earth.

3 To prevent jumping over or climbing the fence, raise the height with trellis panels, or attach weld-mesh panels higher than the fence and leaning inwards at the top. You can thwart keen jumpers by stopping them getting a good run-up to the fence with a line of shrubs or a second, lower fence some 60cm (2ft) inside it.

4 Garden gates should be lockable – latches aren't secure enough, and some dogs learn to operate them.

5 Don't rely on electric fences or 'invisible' fencing (where the dog receives an electric shock from his collar when he attempts to cross the line) if no one is home to monitor your dog. Strong motivation (e.g. high prey drive, the scent of a bitch on heat, sudden panic) can overcome a dog's reluctance to face the pain of an electric shock.

6 An outdoor kennel with a run will keep your dog safely confined for short periods if necessary – but remember that a dog should be a companion, not a prisoner to be incarcerated!

▲ *Once a dog has discovered the fun of bolting, keeping him in becomes increasingly difficult, so put effort into prevention rather than cure.*

HORRIBLE AT HOME

MY DOG CHASES MY CAT

Cause: Cats run, dogs chase – it's an inbuilt instinct. Until you teach your dog to restrain his chase drive and both animals learn to trust each other, instinct will kick in automatically.

Action: Reduce the pressure on your cat to run away by ensuring that he has escape routes and dog-proof refuges in every room. At the same time, work on teaching your dog his basic exercises – Sit, Stay, Come, Leave it – in increasingly distracting situations, until he is rock steady on ignoring the cat and paying attention to you instead. If necessary, use a house-line (a long trailing lead) so you can physically prevent him from zooming off after the cat instead of sitting down when told. This two-fold approach aims to reduce the dog's stimulus to chase by reducing the cat's urge to run away, at the same time as teaching the dog to control his chase instincts. Increasing the time spent on your dog's training will also help to keep his mind occupied so that he has less interest in chasing. When the two animals can ignore each other, leave it to them to decide if they wish to become friends – often they will.

Prevention: When introducing a new dog to the household, initially keep him on the lead in the cat's presence, checking any attempts to approach the cat and rewarding him for ignoring the cat and paying attention to you. Only allow him free range alongside the cat once you are sure that he has understood the rules.

HOW DO I INTRODUCE A NEW KITTEN TO MY DOG?

Action: Unless your dog is already used to cats and knows better than to bounce at small pets, it is generally safest to keep dog and kitten in separate rooms for at least two days. This gives the kitten time to make himself at home and relax. Once he is settled, switch the animals round, letting the dog into the kitten's room while releasing the kitten to explore the rest of the house so that, while still physically separated, they are able to familiarise themselves with each other's scent. How soon you make direct introductions will depend on how your dog reacts. If he is frantically excited by the kitten's smell, wait a few more days until he is calmer.

Before introducing the two animals, plan ahead: make sure the kitten has an escape route (a baby gate across a doorway, fixed high enough for a kitten to scoot underneath, is useful). Settle yourself in the chosen room with your dog on leash and a handful of treats, and invite the kitten in. With a gentle dog, the introduction should go easily; with a bouncy dog or a keen hunter, you will have to spend a lot of time teaching him kitty manners.

◀ *Dogs and cats in the same home can become devoted friends.*

Some misunderstandings are to be expected at first, so supervise all encounters closely to protect both parties. Never leave the two animals alone together until you are sure that they are good friends. Remember that dogs tend to investigate with their noses, and kittens tend to swat nearby objects – it is all too easy for sharp little claws to injure a dog's eyes.

MY DOG VIEWS MY PET RABBIT AS PREY

Cause: Natural hunting instinct.
Breed notes: Most dogs can be taught to live in harmony with what they would normally consider prey animals, but it is a lot harder to teach dogs

with a strong hunting drive, such as terriers.
Action: Protect your rabbit! Ensure not only that his hutch and run are dog-proof, but also that they are situated where your dog cannot cause him stress by huffing and puffing through the wires. Then work on your dog's basic obedience training and in particular on the 'Leave it' exercise – it pays to spend time teaching him that it is rewarding to focus his attention on you before you work on the rabbit problem. Only when he is responsive in the face of distractions generally is it fair (or worthwhile) to practise, on leash, within sight and smell of the rabbit. If your dog's hunting drive is not overpowering, in time training will win out over instinct. However, some dogs will never be trustworthy with small animals if you are not there to supervise them.
Prevention: Dogs which are brought up with smaller pets from puppyhood, with firm guidelines laid down from day one, will usually co-exist happily with them. However, unless you have absolute confidence in your dog, it is best to keep temptation out of his way and ensure that your rabbit (or other small pet) is always securely out of reach in your absence.

▼ *It's natural for dogs to chase prey animals. With patience and supervision, some dogs can become trustworthy with small pets – others do not.*

HORRIBLE AT HOME

SHOULD I GET A SECOND DOG?

The answer depends on you, your dog, and your lifestyle. Dogs are social animals who enjoy being part of a pack, but they can be perfectly happy with their owners without the need for canine company at home. If you are thinking of acquiring a second dog because you don't have enough time for your present dog and feel he is lonely, think again – you won't have time for the new dog either, and two dogs left to their own devices mean trouble. Similarly, don't consider a second dog as a solution to any behavioural problems your present dog may have, as bad habits are catching.

The only good reason for getting a second dog is that you genuinely want two dogs and have the time, interest and financial resources to look after both of them. Two dogs can be twice the fun, but also twice the commitment in work, time and expense. If you decide to go ahead, do take your dog's personality and reaction to other dogs into account. If he has been your only dog for a long time, or is timid, aggressive, highly territorial or possessive of you, he may regard a newcomer as an unwelcome trespasser and a threat to his lifestyle. However, if you feel that your dog would enjoy a companion, if you choose the new dog

▲ *Dogs of disparate sizes can become buddies, but they will have more fun playing together if they are better matched in stature.*

with care and if you are prepared to put time and effort into encouraging them to get along, a second dog can be a delight – and you could end up being a multi-dog household.

HOW SHOULD I CHOOSE A SECOND DOG?

Think carefully about the most suitable size, gender, age and temperament. Although dogs of very disparate sizes can be good friends, bear in mind that little dogs can suffer accidental injury when playing with big dogs. If you have a bouncy, clumsy adolescent Great Dane, a fragile toy breed puppy stands a high chance of being knocked over, squashed or clonked by a paw bigger than its own head. Gender is important. In general, the happiest combination is that of a dog and a bitch (although you will need to have the bitch spayed to avoid unwanted pregnancies or the turmoil of having to keep them separated twice a year);

with same-sex pairs, there is an increased risk of fights, especially between two bitches, and especially if you choose a high-dominance (e.g. most guard types) or high reactivity (e.g. many terriers) breed.

In terms of age, some older dogs may be too set in their ways to cope with the demands of a mischievous puppy; others may be rejuvenated by the company of a youngster. If your dog is mature,

▲ Dogs benefit from canine company and can gain great enjoyment (as well as increased levels of exercise) from being part of a pack.

an adult rescue dog may be a better companion for him than a puppy. Just as not all human adults are good with children, not all dogs are good with puppies. Some may not have enough patience with puppy misbehaviour, while others may have too much — a gentle, submissive older dog can inadvertently turn an average puppy into a bully. If you do decide to take on a rescue dog, most rescue centres will be able to give you guidance as to how well each of their charges socialises with other canines, and you should be able to take your own pet to meet them and make his own choice of friend.

▶ Two dogs mean extra time commitment to reinforce each dog's relationship with you.

HOW DO I INTRODUCE A SECOND DOG?

Action: If possible, introduce the two dogs on neutral ground, rather than bringing your new dog home and thrusting him into your first dog's territory. The easiest way is to bring them together in the park where they can introduce themselves at leisure and get to know each other before going home together. If your new dog is a puppy, of course he will not be able to go out and about until he has had his vaccinations, so you will have to make the introduction at home. Usually it is best to keep the older dog on a leash initially, so that the puppy is not at risk if he reacts badly.

Don't try and force a friendship; make sure both dogs have a comfortable place to which they can retreat; and don't leave them alone together until you are confident that they are firm friends (which may take days, or even months). Accept that there will be some disagreements while the dogs sort out the dynamics of their relationship. Unless there is real risk of injury, it is best not to interfere but to let the dogs sort it out themselves.

HORRIBLE AT HOME

MULTIPLE DOG HOUSEHOLDS

Two dogs (or more) can be twice as much fun as one – or can mean double trouble. Individual dogs may not necessarily get on together, or may get on all too well and lead each other astray. Multi-dog owners need to be clear about their own role as pack leader and aware of pack dynamics.

MY DOGS WOULD RATHER PLAY WITH EACH OTHER THAN LISTEN TO ME

Cause: It's natural for dogs to enjoy playing with each other, and the multi-dog owner needs to compete with this inclination by building up strong individual bonds with each dog.
Action: Allocate individual time for each dog for play, grooming, and especially for training sessions away from the other dog(s). You need to establish that you are even more rewarding company than another canine, and also that you are the pack leader, with the right to call either or both dogs back from whatever they are doing. Work on the recall of each dog individually, using a reward-based approach. Let the dogs enjoy playtime together, but introduce a cue for 'Yes, it's okay to play now', and another for 'That's enough – stop playing'. The more time you spend on individual obedience training, the more interest they will have in responding to you, and the more control you will have over them.
Prevention: Build up individual bonds with each dog from the start. Don't allow unlimited playtime whenever they choose – interrupt play when you think it has gone on long enough and

▲ *When you have several dogs, it is important that they know you are the pack leader.*

separate the dogs for short periods, giving each an appealing chew toy so that their time apart is also enjoyable.

MY TWO DOGS HAVE STARTED FIGHTING

Cause: Dogs need to establish a rank order, and if this is not clear, they will attempt to settle the matter by fighting. Often problems arise when one or both dogs are maturing and feel ready to challenge for higher status.
Breed notes: Low-dominance breeds (e.g. Cavalier King Charles Spaniel) require less work to keep the peace at home than high-dominance guard breeds (e.g. Akita).
Action: Try to establish which

dog is dominant – check who demands to be first in line to be petted, grabs the favourite sleeping area, pushes ahead of the other dogs through doorways, is the winner in games of tug-of-war and in staring contests, receives most attention from the other dogs, and tends to mount the other dogs (male or female), etc. Now you need to go against the natural human impulse to console the underdog, and instead support the dominant dog in his position – feed him first, pet him first, let him out first, and generally acknowledge his status.

If there is a scrap and the dogs have to be separated, make sure it is the subordinate one who is put out of your presence, not the leader. Don't overdo things by lavishing attention on the top dog and ignoring the other, but make it clear that the top dog receives his share of attention first.

◀ Play-fighting can turn into real fighting and a relationship breakdown if dogs are not sure of their ranking.

The goal is to have both dogs comfortable with their status. Having the underdog neutered will further reinforce the two dogs' rank order. It is also vital to increase the time you spend on training both dogs. The dominant dog needs to learn that, while he holds the top position amongst four-legged members of the family, you are the ultimate chief and will not tolerate misbehaviour; the underdog needs to be equally clear on his position.

Watch your dogs' body language: it is easier to pick up on the first dirty look between them and distract the dominant dog than to break up a fully-fledged fight. It often helps, too, to increase exercise – tired dogs have less energy for squabbles. In severe cases, it is wise to consult a canine behaviourist to ensure the best chance of success. The worst problems arise if both dogs are naturally of similar dominance levels so there is no clear-cut rank order to reinforce. Some dogs (especially if the disagreement is between two bitches) may never agree to live peacefully together, and one may need to be re-housed.

Prevention: Avoid same-sex combinations, especially in dominant guard breeds – a dog and a bitch (the bitch at least being neutered to prevent the need to separate them when she is in season) are more likely to maintain a good relationship than two dogs or two bitches. Establish a firm, consistent pack leadership yourself, and learn to read canine body language so that you can nip disagreements in the bud.

▲ Pay attention to the dominant dog first, and the subordinate dog will be content to wait his turn.

HORRIBLE AT HOME

OBSESSIVE BEHAVIOUR

Dogs are just as prone to neuroses as humans, especially in the increasingly unnatural conditions in which they (and we) live today. Working breeds kept as pets with no outlet for their working drive are particularly prone to developing obsessive habits, sometimes irritating, sometimes positively harmful.

MY DOG LICKS/CHEWS HIMSELF OBSESSIVELY

Causes: Comfort habit (like thumb-sucking or nail-chewing in humans) which turns into obsessive-compulsive behaviour; could be set off by boredom, stress, discomfort (e.g. arthritis, hip dysplasia) or by sore paws (from e.g. contact dermatitis, small cuts, splinter, parasites); may be linked with food allergy or hypothyroidism; can be attention-seeking behaviour.

Breed notes: Toy breeds may tend to enjoy infantile paw-sucking (of a non-damaging nature); severe licking and chewing, to the point of self-mutilation, occurs more often in large breeds, notably Dobermanns, Labradors, Great Danes and Golden Retrievers.

Action: Consult your vet, who can check out physical causes and may also refer you to a behaviourist. In general, you need to reduce your dog's stress level and teach him alternative behaviours.

Avoid scolding and punishment, and instead use distraction (e.g. a food-stuffed toy with a soft filling such as peanut butter or cream cheese, which takes time and effort to extract). Encourage him to enjoy his toys, so that he can redirect his attention to these rather than chewing his own paws. Spend time grooming every day, so that physical comfort comes from a healthy, enjoyable brushing session rather than from obsessive self-grooming – this will also enable you to pick up any physical problems promptly. A change of lifestyle with increased exercise and fun training sessions often helps, as do some alternative therapies, such as massage or Bach flower remedies, and your vet may also wish to prescribe anti-anxiety medication.

If the problem has developed to the stage of self-mutilation, supervise constantly and be ready to interrupt your dog with a distraction. Bandaging, an Elizabethan collar *(right)* or a deterrent spray may be necessary to block your dog's access to the area he chews – ask for your vet's guidance.

Prevention: Happy dogs with an interesting life are less likely to adopt this habit, although there may be a genetic component. If your dog starts licking or chewing himself, take action early on – the longer he is allowed to carry on, the more deep-rooted the obsession will become, and the harder it will be to tackle.

◀ *Provide chew toys in a range of textures to distract your dog from chewing himself.*

taking up agility as a hobby. If the habit is well-established, it is advisable to consult a behaviourist for assistance.

Prevention: Don't choose a dog with a high working drive and expect him to adapt to a low-stimulation lifestyle as a pet! Never play games with your dog that involve him chasing a light. Teach him a wide variety of interesting activities to keep his mind and body occupied in a healthy fashion; provide a range of toys; and remember that he needs plenty of interactive company.

MY DOG CHASES HIS TAIL OBSESSIVELY

Causes: May be caused by pain or discomfort (e.g. from inflamed anal glands, spinal pain, hip dysplasia); can be an attention-seeking behaviour; can be stress-induced, in which case it can become compulsive to the point of self-mutilation.

Breed notes: Bull Terriers and German Shepherds are particularly prone to this problem.

Action: As above.

Prevention: As above.

MY DOG IS FIXATED ON CHASING LIGHTS OR SHADOWS

Causes: Boredom; frustrated working drive; possible neurological problem; opportunity (owners often inadvertently create this problem by encouraging a dog to chase torchlight or the beam from a laser pen as a game).

Breed notes: Border Collies and some terrier breeds are particularly prone to this problem.

Action: Try to distract your dog with a game or training session as soon as this behaviour starts. Increase your dog's level of stimulating activities generally – more walks, more challenging training,

▲ Challenging, high-stimulus activities, such as agility, can be the salvation of a dog with a high working drive who isn't suited to the quiet life.

141

HORRIBLE AT HOME

WHAT EXTRA CARE DOES MY ELDERLY DOG NEED?

Action: As your dog ages, you should adapt his exercise programme and eating habits to suit his advancing years. Little and often is the guideline for both: replacing a long walk by several short ones, and breaking down the daily food ration into several small meals a day, will benefit him. Keeping fit is important in old age, so watch out for any increase or loss of weight, and adjust food quantities accordingly. Keeping the mind alert is also important: don't let your ageing friend vegetate, but provide mental stimulus by continuing training sessions and encouraging him to have fun. However, remember that he needs more sleep than when he was young, and ensure that he has a comfortable bed where he will not be disturbed. Make time for extra grooming, not just for hygienic reasons but to improve circulation and ease stiffness. Finally, if your dog seems to be slowing down or developing health problems, do see your vet – old age may not be the culprit, but there may be some underlying medical cause which will respond to treatment.

MY ELDERLY DOG SEEMS CONFUSED

Cause: Ageing dogs can suffer from senile confusion – what vets term 'canine cognitive dysfunction'. Symptoms include barking for no apparent reason, a disrupted sleep cycle, the development of odd habits (e.g. compulsively scratching at the carpet), progressive loss of memory and a dwindling ability to socialise with people and other dogs.

Action: Do consult your vet. He can prescribe medication to improve blood circulation to the brain, which can alleviate the symptoms; he may also recommend a special diet to help detoxify brain tissue. Remember that old dogs also need extra support and reassurance from their owners to help them cope with physical and mental frailty. They will appreciate a peaceful, orderly

▲ An old dog needs the comfort of undisturbed rest periods in a quiet part of the house.

▲ Like people, dogs slow down with age, and need to take exercise at a gentler pace than youngsters.

household where they are treated with due consideration.

Prevention: There is no prevention for old age, but if you keep life interesting for your dog and exercise his brain with training, he will remain alert longer. Teaching an old dog new tricks is not only possible but advisable – it will help him to function better.

MY ELDERLY DOG IS BECOMING INCONTINENT AT NIGHT

Causes: Liver, kidney or hormonal disease (causing increased drinking therefore increased need to urinate); inappropriate diet (consider changing to a 'senior' diet); ageing bladder sphincter muscle.

Action: See your vet, who can establish the cause of the problem and in many cases provide appropriate medication.

MY ELDERLY DOG IS GOING BLIND AND/OR DEAF

Sight and hearing often deteriorate in older dogs, but most cope well with disability, depending increasingly on their remaining senses, particularly smell, to compensate. You can help your dog in various ways. You can teach your blind dog to follow the sound (and vibration) of a foot tapped on the ground, and make it easier for him to find his way around the house by not changing the layout of furniture. With a deaf dog, you will have to remember to attract his attention by hand gestures or, if he is not looking at you, by touching him. Remember that dogs with failing

▲ *Teaching hand signals as well as voice commands will help later on if your dog's hearing starts to fail.*

senses may not be aware of people approaching them, and may be startled if taken unawares.

They can still enjoy walks, although you will need to keep an eye on them (and keep them on the lead more often) to ensure their safety – blind dogs can't see obstacles, while dogs with failing hearing can't hear the recall and may wander off in the wrong direction. Communication is an important part of our relationship with our dogs, so when their senses fail it is essential to work out alternatives to words or hand gestures. A deaf dog can become depressed in a world where apparently nobody speaks to him any more, and a dog who is both deaf and blind is totally dependent on the sense of touch to receive any input from his owner.

▶ *Most dogs cope with blindness surprisingly well, given a little help.*

DOGGY DAMAGE

We all want a dog who can be relied on not to wreck our home or destroy our belongings, but that doesn't happen automatically. Dogs are designed to chew, and they don't know the difference between our valued possessions and their own toys until we take the time and trouble to teach them.

MY DOG WRECKS MY HOME WHEN I GO OUT

Causes: Separation anxiety (acute distress at being left alone); boredom; stress; surplus energy; lack of training; teething.

Breed notes: Dogs with powerful jaws (e.g. Bull Terriers) are especially prone to chewing, giant breeds can cause a lot of damage through sheer clumsiness, especially while young, and working breeds (e.g. herders and gundogs) are likely to react badly if denied a sufficiently active lifestyle. A recent survey found that the worst offenders were Great Danes and Chihuahuas. Think about it. Neither breed is particularly destructive by nature – but both are often bought as fashion accessories rather than companions. **Any dog which is under-exercised and under-stimulated may become destructive through sheer boredom and frustration.**

Action: First, establish the cause. A dog who appears distressed when you leave and overwhelmingly relieved when you return indicates that the problem is likely to be separation anxiety, which requires systematic desensitisation (*see pp.148-9*). If he is teething (and teething discomfort may continue for some months after the second teeth have come through), he needs to be provided with approved items to chew, and should not be allowed unsupervised access to the whole house – shut him in the kitchen when you go out, or introduce him to a crate, rather than expose him to temptation. If he is neither distressed nor teething, but has simply

◀ *A bored dog, left alone, has to find some means of passing the time!*

been amusing himself dismantling your home, he needs you to put more time and effort into keeping him occupied. Increase exercise to use up his energy – tired dogs are less likely to get into mischief. Institute training sessions every day to occupy his mind and focus him on more desirable activities. Spend time teaching him which items are his toys and can be played with, and which are your possessions and must be left alone. Supervise him closely to prevent him from making mistakes such as chewing chairs – prevention is much less trouble than having to cure a problem. When you go out, leave him something to do in your absence – a food-stuffed toy will keep him occupied, leaving the radio on softly may provide reassurance and prevent him from feeling lonely, or, if you have to leave him for long periods, consider hiring a dog-walker to take him out.

Prevention: Be aware of your dog's needs. Make sure he has a good, stimulating walk before you leave him, spend time on training, and don't expect an intelligent, active animal to do nothing for hours on end.

MY DOG CHEWS EVERYTHING

Causes: Teething puppies chew to ease the discomfort of sore gums; stressed dogs often chew to comfort themselves; and dogs in general enjoy chewing objects – the canine equivalent to watching television!

Action: Whether dealing with a teething puppy or an adult who has not learned acceptable behaviour, you need the same three-step approach: **protect**, **provide** and **correct**. Every time your dog succeeds in chewing your possessions or your furniture, he is learning an enjoyable habit, so it's vital to

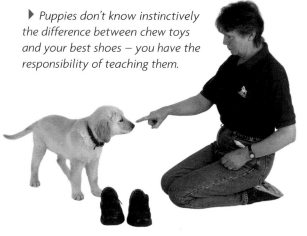

▶ *Puppies don't know instinctively the difference between chew toys and your best shoes – you have the responsibility of teaching them.*

protect them from him. You may have to become obsessively tidy during this period! Put vulnerable objects out of reach, safeguard furniture with taste-deterrent sprays, close doors or use nursery gates to restrict your dog's access to items, and don't allow him the run of the house at any time you cannot supervise his activities. Be sure to **provide** him with appropriate chew toys *(below)* – don't confuse him by giving him an old shoe as a toy and then telling him off when he assumes that all shoes are toys! He will value his toys more if you and he spend time playing with them together – this will also make them more comforting to him in your absence, as the toys acquire your smell. Praise him when he chews his own toys; quietly but firmly **correct** him when he starts to chew anything else. Never chase after him to retrieve whatever he is chewing, but teach him 'No' and 'Leave it', and replace it with one of his own toys.

Prevention: Supervise your new dog from the first day, following this programme. The less often he is allowed to make a mistake, the easier it is to teach desirable behaviour.

DOGGY DAMAGE

MY DOG SCRATCHES THE DOORS

Cause: Dog wants to pass through door, and scratches at it either in an attempt to work his way through, or to signal his need to you *(left)*.

Action: Establish when and why your dog does this. If he is signalling that he needs to go out, teach him an alternative behaviour such as 'Speak' (a single bark at the door). Each time he scratches, tell him 'No', ask him to bark, then open the door. If he is damaging the door while you are out, he may not have had adequate toileting opportunity before you leave (in which case the remedy is obvious), or he may be distressed at your absence *(see pp.148-9 on separation anxiety)*.

Prevention: While tackling the problem, protect your doors with a physical barrier such as a nursery gate, or attach a sheet of sturdy plastic to the bottom of the door (you can buy ready-made door protectors for a tidier appearance).

MY DOG SCRATCHES AT THE FLOORS AND CARPETS

Causes: Misplaced bed-making (dogs have an instinct to scratch and scrape their beds into shape — a wasted effort when directed at bare floors or flat carpets, but a habit hard to break); floor scratching may also be stimulated by an exciting smell or noise (e.g. old food spills invisible to us, or the sound of water-pipes or mice under the floorboards), or by irritation in the feet.

Action: Protect the area of floor where your dog does this. You can cover it with a small sheet of corrugated plastic to make an unpleasant-feeling surface, or, if you have a dedicated chewer who might eat the plastic, move your furniture to cover vulnerable places. You may need to shut your dog out of certain rooms when you are not available to supervise. Check for attractants, such as mice under the floor, and clean the area with pet-repellant spray or lemon juice diluted in warm water to remove any

▶ *Provide cushions and blankets so your dog can enjoy bed-making.*

lingering smells. Inspect your dog's feet for any sign of irritation or overgrown nails. Supervise your dog, and distract him the moment he starts scratching. Directing him to his own bed where he has a blanket that he can scratch and paw into place is often a successful distraction.

▲ *Overgrown nails are uncomfortable for your dog as well as causing damage to floors.*

Prevention: Discourage this activity whenever it starts, offering your dog an alternative such as his own blanket. Don't leave an untrained dog unsupervised in a room with vulnerable floors.

MY DOG DRAGS CUSHIONS OFF CHAIRS

Causes: Cushions make great beds and fun toys, unless you teach your dog that this is not what they are for. If a normally well-behaved bitch starts dragging your cushions around, suspect a false pregnancy or other hormonal upset.
Action: Supervise your dog, and be there to say 'No!' when he does this. If he is prone to taking your cushions when you are out, remove them from the room he is in before you leave. You can spray cushions with pungent-smelling repellant, or cover sofas and chairs with prickly strips (available from pet-shops) to discourage an approach. Make sure your dog has a comfortable bed and suitable toys so that he has no need to borrow your cushions.
Prevention: As above.

MY DOG CHEWS UP THE INSIDE OF THE CAR

Causes: Anxiety; boredom; excitement; teething.
Action: Accustom your dog to travelling in a crate within the car, providing him with an attractive chew or food-stuffed toy to keep him occupied. You may need to spend time ensuring that he is comfortable with car rides and not anxious (*see pp.108-9*).
Prevention: Don't leave your dog to his own devices in the car. Either train him to relax in a crate, or ensure that you have a passenger to supervise him.

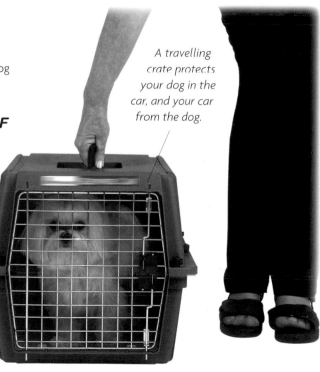

A travelling crate protects your dog in the car, and your car from the dog.

▲ *Your dog should never be put in a position where he can damage the inside of your vehicle. For his own safety, he should always be restrained or supervised by a passenger while in the car.*

147

DOGGY DAMAGE

UNDERSTANDING SEPARATION ANXIETY

Dogs are social creatures. They aren't designed to cope with being alone – this is a skill they have to learn. If we don't give them the opportunity to learn this, they can suffer acute distress (separation anxiety) when left on their own, which often leads to behaviour causing their owners equal distress. Symptoms include following you from room to room, becoming upset when you leave *(right)*, distraught behaviour in your absence (destructiveness, crying and howling, and/or loss of control of bowels), and frenzied greetings when you return. Separation anxiety is commonest in rescue dogs who carry emotional baggage and fear being abandoned again, but can also be caused by a change in lifestyle (e.g. house move, death of a family member or owner increasing work hours). There is no 'quick fix' – it takes time for a dog to develop this level of insecurity, and it takes time to overcome it.

MY DOG IS DISTRESSED WHEN I GO OUT

Cause: See above.

Action: Desensitise your dog to your departure by repeatedly going through the motions. Ignoring the dog, put on your coat, pick up your bag and your house keys, go to the door, then turn round, take off your coat and carry on with some household task. Go through the whole routine again a few minutes later – and again, and again.

▶ *A happy, well-balanced dog may be disappointed when you go out without him, but not distressed – he should be able to cope with your absence.*

Once your dog stops responding to that, take the procedure a stage further and actually leave the house, count to 15, and come back. Increase the time you are out of the house in very gradual stages, never moving on until your dog is completely ignoring your actions. Keep your attitude matter-of-fact, don't respond to your dog's reactions, and don't make a fuss of him when you come in (just make eye contact and say 'Hi', before turning your attention to taking off your coat). You will need to take the time to do this several times every day, and a severe case may take weeks to be resolved, but it is well worth it for your dog's (and your own) peace of mind.

Prevention: Accustom a new dog to being left for short periods from the start, popping out for a minute several times a day and building up the time gradually.

MY DOG FOLLOWS ME ALL AROUND THE HOUSE

Cause: Over-dependence upon owner.

Breed notes: Dogs bred to be close companions (e.g. Cavalier King Charles Spaniels) can tend to be clingy, as can some working breeds designed to work closely with owners (herders, some gundogs).

Action: Clingy dogs lack confidence, and will be happier if you teach them to be more independent. Start obedience training so that you can teach your dog to sit-stay at an increasing distance from you within the home. Don't let him demand attention by pawing and whining, but give him lots of opportunities to earn it through training and play. Schedule daily periods when he is separated from you by a nursery gate through which he can see and hear you, and chat to him calmly while you carry out some activity unconnected with him. Don't try to reassure him, which is more likely to confirm his worries than allay them. A chew or a food-stuffed toy may help to occupy him while you are in another room. Gradually accustoming him to the idea that the world doesn't end if he isn't glued to your ankles won't make him less loving, but will produce a happier,

◀ *Dependent, clingy dogs may seem very appealing, but they will find life much less stressful if they can learn to stand on their own four paws.*

more secure dog who is less likely to suffer from separation anxiety if you have to leave him for a while.

Prevention: Make a regular point of leaving your dog in one room for a few minutes while you are elsewhere in the house, particularly when he is sleepy after a walk, or engaged with a chew, to teach him that separation does not mean abandonment.

MY DOG IS DISTRESSED WHEN LEFT ALONE

Cause: Over-dependence – in rescue dogs often caused by owners over-compensating for their pet's sad past, encouraging him to need extra attention all the time.

Action: Start the slow process of desensitising your dog against your departure and teaching him to cope with separation, as above. In severe cases, you may need the help of a behaviourist who can formulate a re-education programme for you. It may also be helpful to use a pheromone diffuser (available from vets and some pet stores), which contains a calming scent based on the smell of a puppy's mother.

Prevention: Encourage some independence from the start, and practise short periods of separation.

DOGGY DAMAGE

MY DOG DIGS UP THE GARDEN

Cause: Dogs like digging. They dig to hunt mice, moles and other small wildlife; to bury bones and other treasures; to scrape out a comfortable bed; and just for fun.

Breed notes: Terriers *(below)* – the name meaning 'earth dogs'! – and Dachshunds in particular are born to dig.

Action: Accompany your dog into the garden so that you are there to supervise and interrupt any misbehaviour as soon as it starts. Fill in any holes already dug and cover them with stones to prevent the culprit from returning to them, and protect tempting areas of soft earth with wire netting.

Prevention: Don't leave your dog alone in the garden until you have established a good pattern of behaviour.

MY DOG TRACKS PATHS THROUGH MY FLOWERBEDS

Cause: Dogs like to patrol their territory, and they don't know that flowerbeds are to be avoided unless you teach them.

Action: Train your dog to keep off the flowerbeds, taking him into the garden on an extending lead and tweaking him back with a firm 'No' whenever he sets a paw on the border, praising him when he keeps to acceptable routes. Putting up temporary (or indeed permanent) low fencing around the flowerbeds will make it easier for him to learn. It may be worthwhile setting up little paths, covered with wood chips or gravel, especially for his use round the back of the border out of sight, so that he can enjoy a border patrol and you can enjoy your flowers undamaged.

▶ *Flowers and dogs can co-exist– plan well to enjoy both.*

Where a dog has already established a favourite route across the flowerbeds, it may be easiest to give in and make a feature of this by laying stepping stones. In both cases you will need to supervise his use of these paths at first so that he learns to keep off the flowers.

Prevention: Never leave a puppy or new dog alone and unwatched in the garden to do as he pleases – time spent establishing where he can go and where he can't is a good investment.

▶ *If you combine gardening with dog-training, you can build up your relationship teaching your puppy his 'Stay' and 'Leave it' commands as part of your routine.*

MY PUPPY KEEPS UPROOTING MY PLANTS

Causes: Play – it's fun to pull up plants and carry them around. Puppies may also have a strong innate retrieving instinct that urges them to fetch things indoors to you.

Action: Take your puppy into the garden and let

▲ *Pouring water over the area where your dog has just urinated will make your lawn less smelly, and prevent the urine from damaging the grass.*

him watch you replace the plants, using the 'No' command (and, if necessary, an extending lead) to make it clear that these are not to be touched. Immediately afterwards, encourage him to find an alternative approved article (e.g. a toy, a glove, a handkerchief) in the garden and praise him for

picking that up. With repeated practice, he will learn that some items are to be played with and others, including your plants, are to be left alone.

Prevention: Supervise and educate your dog in the garden from day one.

DOG URINE LEAVES BROWN PATCHES ON MY LAWN

Cause: Canine urine is a mild fertiliser which normally does no harm to plants, but when concentrated in one area its salt content (urea) will burn foliage. Bitches are usually more of a problem when it comes to lawn damage, simply because male dogs are more likely to lift a leg on a tree than squat down to water the grass.

Action: Cordon off damaged sections of lawn to give them time to recover. When you see your dog urinating on the grass, tip a full watering can over the area immediately. This will dilute the urine so that it merely acts as a fertiliser and does the grass good instead of burning it. Beware of tips to put additives of any kind in your dog's food or water – some may not work, and some are actively harmful. For example, one common suggestion is to add tomato ketchup to the dog's diet. This often works, but at a cost to the dog's health: the salt in the ketchup makes the dog thirsty, so he drinks more and therefore produces more diluted urine – and it also carries a risk of damaging his kidneys.

Prevention: Train your dog to empty his bladder in an approved spot in the garden other than the lawn; water the lawn frequently; or consider re-sowing your lawn with a tougher grass, such as fescue.

TOP TIPS

THE NEW PUPPY

1 Plan ahead – everything from sleeping arrangements to holiday schemes.

2 The more time you spend on his early education, the less work you will have to put in later.

3 Start as you mean to go on: don't encourage behaviour (e.g. jumping up) which won't be welcome when your puppy is an adult.

4 Socialise (but don't swamp) your pup from the start. Even before he is vaccinated, you can carry him out and about in your arms to introduce him to new sights and sounds.

5 Practise grooming, handling paws, ears and inspecting teeth and gums, every day.

DIET

1 Stick to regular mealtimes – four times a day for puppies under 12 weeks, then three times a day until they are six months old, and twice daily thereafter.

2 Feed your dog appropriately for his age and activity level. Don't choose a high-energy diet for a dog who only potters round the park!

3 Count treats as well as meals when calculating your dog's daily intake.

4 Watch your dog's waistline and adjust food quantities as necessary.

5 Read the list of ingredients when buying dog-food to avoid foods with lots of additives.

COLLARS AND LEADS

1 A collar should be comfortable. Soft leather is always a safe bet. Avoid stiff, hard collars or styles which cause pain (check chains, prong collars, electric shock collars are not appropriate).

2 Head-collars and no-pull harnesses are better than collars for dogs who pull, increasing your control and avoiding damage to the dog's neck.

3 Head-collars must be properly fitted. Badly fitted head-collars may slip up into the eyes or come off altogether.

4 Extending leads are great for training sessions but inappropriate when walking near traffic or where people can be tripped up by them.

5 Trigger-style lead-clips are safest, to avoid accidentally pinching your dog (or your fingers), but check clips regularly for wear.

EXERCISE

1 Don't over-walk puppies. Two 15-minute walks a day are enough for a young puppy, building up to two 30-minute walks when he is six months old and gradually increasing until he is mature.

2 Don't under-walk adult dogs. The average adult dog needs at least two half-hour walks every day, often much more.

3 Schedule time for free running as well as for leashed walks. Your

dog needs both to achieve maximum fitness.

4 Take care when exercising physically exaggerated breeds. Discourage long-backed dogs from jumping or running up and down stairs; don't over-strain short-legged or short-muzzled breeds.

5 Check paws after a walk. Embedded grass seeds or minor cuts need tackling immediately.

GOOD WALKING MANNERS

1 Make sure your dog is always under control, either leashed or trained to come back when called. Keep your attention on him so that he can't get into mischief – or danger.

2 Keep your dog on the leash where livestock is about – better safe than sorry.

3 Don't let your dog be a nuisance to other people or their dogs.

4 Don't let people pet your dog without permission. He may not like it, or he may like it too much and start demanding attention from every passer-by.

5 Always carry poo-bags and clean up after your dog has defecated.

WEATHER

1 Overheating can kill. Make sure your dog has access to shade in summer, and don't walk him in the heat of a summer day.

2 Dogs die if left in hot cars – and also in freezing vehicles.

3 Thick fur provides good insulation from the cold for many dogs, but fine-coated breeds need winter warmers (coats, blankets, etc.).

4 Damp causes damage to joints – always dry your dog after a wet walk.

5 Ice (and salt or grit on the ice) is bad for paws – always rinse your dog's feet after an icy walk.

TRAINING

1 Rewards (toys, titbits, petting) encourage learning – punishment (smacking, shouting) dulls your dog's attention.

2 Repetition and consistency are needed. Little and often is better than occasional long sessions.

3 Don't set yourself (and your dog) up for failure by trying to teach commands when he is likely to disobey. Repeated commands that you can't enforce teach your dog to ignore you.

4 Compete with distractions by making yourself more interesting.

5 Practise in different places and different situations. Dogs often learn that they have to walk to heel at the training class, without extending this lesson to other areas.

INDEX

INDEX

INDEX

PICTURE CREDITS

Bayer HealthCare: 49 bottom left.
Bigstockphoto.com
Andraz Cerar: 53 bottom right.
Pattie: 48 top.
Jiri Vaclavek: 57 right.
Jane Burton, Warren Photographic: Front cover main image, 4 bottom, 23 centre left, 42 both, 50, 52, 60 top, 62, 63 top, 64 top left, 76, 82 top, 82 bottom (dog), 84 bottom, 85 right, 86 bottom, 89 bottom (dog), 120 left, 139 top, 140 top left, 140 bottom, 145 bottom.
Crestock.com
Marc Dietrich: 57 left.
Goh Siok Hian: 29 bottom left.
Eric Isselée: 51 bottom.
Michael Pettigrew: 29 bottom right.
Varina and Jay Patel: 79 bottom.
Lisa F. Young: 111 top.
Dusan Zidar: Back cover rt inset, 28 centre rt.
Philip de Ste. Croix: 60 bottom.
Dreamstime.com
Aaleksander: Back cover centre left, 111 centre left.
Yuri Arcurs: Back cover top right, 75 top.
Karen Arnold: 100 bottom left.
Judy Benjoud: 111 bottom.
Lon Dean; 101.
Tom Dowd: 132 top.
EastWest Imaging: 72 bottom.
Dewayne Flowers: 40 top.
Frenc: 33 bottom.
Scott Griessel: 61.
Jostein Hauge: 75 bottom.
Eric Isselée: 81 right.
Jxpfeer: 99.
Kitsen: 146 centre right.
Tammy Mcallister: 33 centre right.
Denise Mcquillen: 100 top.
Christine Nichols: 13 bottom.
Raycan: 77 bottom, 131 bottom.
Showface: 49 bottom right.
Sunheyy: 95 bottom.
Eti Swinford: 83.
Marzanna Syncerz: 79 top.
Teekaygee: 94 top.
Lisa Turay: 34 top.
Anke Van Wyk: 6 top right, 64 centre left.
Fotolia.com
Yuri Arcurs: 148 bottom.
Hagit Berkovich: 46 top left.
Callalloo Alexis: 9 bottom.
Callalloo Twisty: 119 top.
Lars Christensen: 73 top right.
CPJ Photography: 65 bottom.
Cynoclub: 77 top left.
Dagel: 47, 133 bottom right.
Melanie DeFazio: 86 top.
Jaimie Duplass 58.
EastWest Imaging: 7 bottom right.
Eric Isselée: 70 bottom left, 144.
Svetlana Larina: 35 top.
Steve Lovegrove: 110.
Mikhail Lukyanov: 38 top.
Maciej Qn Majewski: 151 centre left.

Marea: 77 centre right.
Igor Norman: 9 top right.
Jelena Popic: 72 centre left.
Martina Reimers: 4 top, 113 centre right.
Paul Retherford: 59 top.
Roberto72: 87 right.
Saniphoto: 5 centre left, 29 top.
Gleb Semenjuk: 8 bottom right.
Annette Shaff: 78.
Southmind: 27 bottom right.
Lisa Turay: 31 centre left.
Elliot Westacott: 28 bottom left.
Interpet Publishing Archive: Front cover top right, back cover bottom left, 1 centre, 4 left, 8 top left, 10, 15 bottom right, 16, 17 left, 23 bottom right, 24, 25 top, 26, 30 both, 32, 36 top (bags), 39, 41 both, 44 top, 46 bottom, 51 top, 53 bottom left, 54, 55 top, 59 right, 66, 67, 68, 69, 70 centre sequence, 71, 73 centre left, 82 bottom (child), 84 top, 89 right, 91 top, 95 top, 96 all, 97 all, 100 bottom right, 102 bottom, 117 bottom, 118, 120 bottom, 122 bottom, 124, 125 bottom, 127, 129, 130, 139 bottom, 143 top, 145 top, 147 top, 147 bottom, 148 top.
iStockphoto.com
Ana Abejon: 5 top, 7 left.
Aldra: Front cover bottom left.
Alija: 6 top left.
Anyka: Front cover bottom right.
Cristian Ardelean: 17 bottom left, 126 top left.
Maria Bibikova: 14.
Joshue Blake: 88 bottom.
Daniel Bobrowski: 15 top.
Emmanuelle Bonzami: 87 bottom.
Byron Carlson: 37 top right.
Willee Cole: 122 top.
Ben Conlan: 19 right.
DigitalHarold: 45 bottom.
ad_doward: 21 top right.
espion: 21 centre right.
Rob Fox: 149.
Jean Frooms: 93 bottom.
Hedda Gjerpen: 11, 137 bottom.
Joanna Green: 94 left.
HannamariaH: 150 right, 151 top.
Mandy Hartfree-Bright: 12.
Michelle Harvey: 93 top right.
Greg Henry: 142 bottom left.
Uschi Hering: 18.
Stephanie Horrocks: 117 top.
Thomas Hottner: 36 top (sign).
Ken Hurst: 98 top.
Eric Isselée: 136, 143 bottom.
Henk Jelsma: 150 top left.
Jeridu: 49 top.
Mike Jones: 17 centre left.
Joseph C. Justice Jr: 31 bottom right, 133 top.
Oliver Sun Kim: 48 top inset.
Peter Kim: 98 bottom.
Igor Kovalenko: 131 top left.
Aleksey Krylov: 113 top.
Erik Lam: 3 bottom, 90 centre left, 126 top right, 126 bottom, 131 centre (dog).
Athena Lamberis: 147 top (wood).

Michael Ledray: 40 bottom left.
Rich Legg: 140 centre right.
Warwick Lister-Kaye: 4 centre, 116.
Sean Locke: 119 centre.
Pavle Marjanovic: 22.
Gary Martin: 106.
Ivan Mayes: 37 bottom.
Dennis Minix: 33 top.
Hannu Mononen: 137 top left.
Iztok Nok: 141.
Saso Novoselic: 128 top.
PK-Photos: 74.
Alex Potemkin: 40 bottom right.
Leigh Schindler: 55 bottom, 64 top right.
Annette Shaff: 6 bottom.
Grant Shimmin: 90 bottom right.
Joop Snijder: 142 bottom right.
Lisa Svara: 128 bottom.
Todd Taulman: 112 top centre.
Temelko Temelkov: 138.
Jan Tyler: 45 top right.
Frank van den Bergh: 25 bottom.
Anna Utekhina: 88 top.
Annett Vauteck: 15 bottom left.
Jacob Wackerhausen: 89 bottom (couple).
Walik: 131 top right.
Dan Wilton: 13 top.
Monika Wisniewska: 93 top left, 108 left.
Nicole S. Young: 63 bottom.
PetSTEP Inc.: 92.
Shutterstock.com
Aceshot1: 114 bottom.
AVAVA: 19 left, 38 bottom left.
Gualberto Becerra: 35 centre left.
Hagit Berkovich: 153 top.
Heidi Brand: 114 top left.
Dmitrijs Dmitrijevs: 153 bottom.
Kevin Duffy: 146 top left.
Jaimie Duplass: 34 bottom left, 80.
Jean Frooms: 5 bottom left, 43, 105 bottom.
Gelpi: 44 bottom left.
Gorilla: 20 top.
Andrew Howard: 121 bottom left.
Eric Isselée: 109 left.
Danger Jacobs: 109 bottom right.
Verity Johnson: 103 right.
Kelis: 115 bottom.
Rolf Klebsattel: 103 top left.
Marina Krasnorutskaya: 107 top.
Michal Napartowicz: 102 top.
Tomas Pavelka: 56 bottom.
Miko Pernjakovic: 1 inset, 3 inset, 85 bottom left.
Quayside: 56 top.
Tina Rencelj: 15 top.
Salamanderman: 27 bottom left.
Jorge Salcedo: 135 centre left.
Sparkling Moments Photography: 20 left.
SV Lumagraphica: 109 top.
Dragan Trifunovic: 80-81.
Tomasz Trojanowski: 27 top.
Simone van den Berg: 123, 152 bottom.
Anke Van Wyk: 112 top left.
Elliot Westacott: 91 bottom right, 121 top, 122 top left, 152 top.
Yuriy Zelenenkyy: 104-5.